Graceful
Influence

Graceful Influence

Making a
Lasting Impact through
Lessons from
Women of the Bible

Lori Stanley Roeleveld

Our Daily Bread
Publishing.

Graceful Influence: Making a Lasting Impact through Lessons from Women of the Bible
© 2024 by Lori Stanley Roeleveld

Interior design by Michael J. Williams

Library of Congress Cataloging-in-Publication Data

Names: Roeleveld, Lori Stanley, author.
Title: Graceful influence : making a lasting impact through lessons from women of the Bible / Lori Stanley Roeleveld.
Description: Grand Rapids, MI : Our Daily Bread Publishing, [2024] | Summary: "Realize the power of your influence by studying biblical women. In 30 short chapters, discover how their choices allowed them to influence generations"-- Provided by publisher.
Identifiers: LCCN 2023036917 (print) | LCCN 2023036918 (ebook) | ISBN 9781640702820 (paperback) | ISBN 9781640702875 (epub)
Subjects: LCSH: Women in the Bible. | BISAC: RELIGION / Christian Living / Women's Interests | RELIGION / Christian Living / Spiritual Growth
Classification: LCC BS575 .R5858 2024 (print) | LCC BS575 (ebook) | DDC 220.9/2082--dc23/eng/20230927
LC record available at https://lccn.loc.gov/2023036917
LC ebook record available at https://lccn.loc.gov/2023036918

Printed in United States of America
24 25 26 27 28 29 30 31 / 8 7 6 5 4 3 2 1

Contents

Contents

To all the Bible study–goers—
the women (and men) so hungry for God's Word
you read it even when no one is looking. You are
not hidden. His eyes are on you always.

Martha, Mary, and This Book

She said to him, "Yes, Lord; I believe that you are the
Christ, the Son of God, who is coming into the world."

John 11:27

We owe Martha an apology.

All of us who have judged her by a single moment, just one exchange in her relationship with Jesus, need to step back and remember that Martha was a woman loved by God. She was created to know and enjoy Him, not to be an object lesson in a thousand sermons, not to become a byword for busyness. Especially not when, too often, we withhold the rest of Martha's story.

Martha and her sister, Mary, welcomed Jesus and the disciples into their home. While Martha busied herself with all the details of serving, driving herself to distraction, Mary sat listening to Jesus speak.

Clearly annoyed, Martha asked Jesus if He even cared that Mary had left her alone to serve. She asked Him to tell her sister to help. "But the Lord answered her, 'Martha, Martha, you are anxious and troubled about many things, but one thing is necessary. Mary has chosen the good portion, which will not be taken from her'" (Luke 10:41–42).

From this single moment, people have done a lot of preaching about the importance of not "being a Martha." The problem is that Jesus didn't tell Martha to stop being Martha, and He didn't say, "Mary's a better person than you are." Jesus invited Martha to look at the choice Mary made, the better one, and to do the same. He didn't condemn Martha; He invited her to focus on Him, not on the busyness ratcheting up her anxiety.

Yes, depending on how it's read, it *can* sound as if Jesus scolded Martha, but what if He did? Jesus once scolded Peter— "he rebuked Peter and said, 'Get behind me, Satan! For you are not setting your mind on the things of God, but on the things of man'" (Mark 8:33).

Now, that's a scolding. That's a rebuke. But I've never seen a Bible study or heard a sermon titled "Be a John, Don't Be a Peter." Peter went on to make even worse decisions than the one that earned him that rebuke, but after His resurrection, Jesus asked Peter to feed His sheep.

Peter changed. He matured in faith. So did Martha.

We see this when Lazarus died. The sisters had sent for Jesus when Lazarus fell sick, but He didn't come immediately. When He did arrive, Martha left her home (and, presumedly, all the tasks of a mourning household) to meet Him.

She expressed her faith in Him even at this time of loss and received not only Jesus's assurance that her brother would rise again but the revelation that Jesus is life. "I am the resurrection and the life. Whoever believes in me, though he die, yet shall he live, and everyone who lives and believes in me shall never die. Do you believe this?" (John 11:25–26).

That's the important question. That's *the* life-changing choice. Do you believe that Jesus is the resurrection and the life? Will you follow Him? Whether you start paying attention to Him immediately, like Mary did, or it takes you a little more time, like it did Martha, what matters is that you do enter into a relationship with Him and allow that relationship to inform your life.

Jesus loved Martha, and He loves you. This love leads us to

want to live in ways that lead toward Him, not away. The Bible is our resource for learning how to take and remain on that wise path, but it's a process. When we follow Jesus, it is *He*—not our sins—who defines us.

The Bible is full of sinners who need Jesus. We try to make them into heroes and saints, but the Word resists that urge. The Holy Spirit inspired the biblical writers to record the sins and weaknesses of most people in Scripture right along with their triumphs. They were imperfect people following a great God, just as we are.

It's not our job to categorize those who came before us. Jezebel isn't a villain and Ruth isn't a saint. Like us, they were sinners surrounded by other sinners making choices in a sinful world. We may struggle to relate to their culture or their situations, but they were people like us.

And clearly, we need Jesus's direction in our decisions. Martha's behavior seems logical on the surface. Many behaviors make sense to us by worldly measures. Without Jesus, we wouldn't see that Mary's choice was toward Jesus while Martha's drew her from Him. Naomi's bitterness (Ruth 1:20) at the loss of her husband and sons is understandable, but it was drawing her away from God, whereas Ruth's mindset in loss drew her toward God. We need the Holy Spirit to help us see the better way.

Women of the Bible lived flesh-and-blood lives of hard work and heartache. Longings and laughter. Fear and faith. Struggles and successes. They existed in a place and time. Consider the women in your life. Each is unique and yet so like the others. Each has her share of pain and a measure of joy. Each is fearfully and wonderfully made. We would never imagine that any of them were created solely to serve as an illustration for the rest of us.

The Bible gives us just a snapshot of people's lives. We gain insight from their stories and their relationships with God, just as we learn from one another. But we must not flatten them into one-dimensional figures or pit them against one another, as people so often have done with Mary and Martha. Martha wasn't less loved by Jesus when she chose poorly, any more than she was more loved by Jesus when she chose well. Neither are we (Romans 8:38–39).

Just as Jesus directed Martha to learn from Mary, we can observe people in the Bible, note the consequences of their actions, and learn. As we look at these women, we'll stay close to the biblical narrative, which is often spare of details. There will be times when we'll use what we know of human nature to cautiously speculate, but God has given us what we need to know. Often, we can learn more than one lesson from their stories. For the sake of this book, I've focused on just one lesson from each woman.

Remember that, like these women, you too are an influencer. We don't always feel influential, but the truth is that ordinary decisions we make will, over time, impact others directly and indirectly. From wearing an "I Voted" sticker to ordering dessert because our friends do, from spreading infectious laughter and contagious yawns to passing on everything from germs to recycling habits, we influence others all the time.

Our choices matter. Our actions have ripple effects, sometimes for generations. We don't have to be powerful leaders, eloquent spokespeople, or recognized personalities to leave legacies. The graceful influence of an ordinary life marked by wise, godly decisions emits light that diminishes the world's darkness.

All Christians have sins from which we've repented and turned. As the saying goes, Jesus followers aren't perfect; we're forgiven and redeemed. We all need Jesus. We all need grace, but we also can exercise graceful influence.

This book isn't intended to be an exhaustive compendium of all the women mentioned in Scripture. You'll find mention of over 120 women, although one or two of your favorites may not be featured (Jephthah, for instance, from Judges, Naaman's wife's servant girl in 2 Kings, and Lois and Eunice in 2 Timothy).

You'll also note that all the choices, even those with negative effect, are presented in context. We live and act in a broken world surrounded by other broken people and cultures. For example, Sarah sent Hagar to Abraham (Genesis 16) to bear a child. That act continues to affect us even now. But Hebrews 11:11 commends Sarah's faith despite her troubled relationships, despite confusion about how God would work, despite her failings.

We live by faith, not by our own righteousness. We are to put no confidence "in the flesh" but in Jesus Christ, "and be found in him, not having a righteousness of my own that comes from the law, but that which comes through faith in Christ, the righteousness from God that depends on faith" (Philippians 3:9). Our confidence is not in the perfection of our lives but in the work of Jesus in us and through us. That is the spirit in which we will explore all actions taken by the women in this book (and yours as well).

There are attitudes that lead toward God and attitudes that lead away from Him. With the power of the Holy Spirit in Christ, we are free to make godly decisions, but we don't always. That's not an excuse, but it is the truth of making our way in a world still marked by sin and death. So we'll exercise compassion.

As we consider these women, if we pay close attention, we'll see God at work in their lives. We'll see His love and mercy for them, and we'll see hope for ourselves in Christ. If we have a relationship with Jesus, He is the final word on all the rest of our decisions. If we haven't chosen a relationship with Him, we're dismissing the choice that makes all the difference, the one that leads to eternal life.

God included a variety of stories of women in the Bible. We can see ourselves in their struggles to know and obey God. We will see ourselves in their challenges, tragedies, and triumphs. They mattered. So do we. British theologian G. K. Chesterton wrote in his Father Brown series: "All men matter. You matter. I matter. It's the hardest thing in theology to believe."[1]

You see, our greatest problem isn't that we don't matter; it's that we do. It isn't that we aren't significant but that our significance is hidden from us by the enemy of God, by life, and by our own doubts.

No matter how small we may feel our lives are or how limited we view our reach, our actions touch and ripple through other lives. We make a difference. We should worry less about the size of our reach and focus more on ensuring our effect is for God's glory.

We influence others because that's how God designed life to work. The only real question is whether our actions will lead toward God or away, will be harmful or graceful. In Christ, the final word on our impact can be unimaginably glorious. Let's listen carefully to some of the women recorded in His Word and let their voices and choices influence ours.

The Woman Devoted to Jesus

The Impact of Love

Truly, I say to you, wherever this gospel is proclaimed in the whole world, what she has done will also be told in memory of her.

Matthew 26:13

Simon was hosting a dinner, and Jesus and His disciples were present with him there in Bethany. It was just before Passover, and soon swelling crowds would congest the streets of nearby Jerusalem. The room buzzed with guests reclining at the table. People of fine reputation served the meal. Everyone's focus was on the honored guest, the rabbi from Galilee.

One woman walked past them all, guests and servers, her attention entirely on Jesus. When she reached Him, she broke open an alabaster flask of costly, pure nard.

Nard (or spikenard) is an oil derived from a plant in the honeysuckle family. It's amber colored, with a musky, woodsy scent. The contents of this woman's flask were aromatic and of great worth, the equivalent of almost a year's wages, perhaps representing her dowry or her life's savings.

Nard is mentioned in the Song of Solomon. The bride says, "While the king was on his couch, my nard gave forth its fragrance" (Song of Solomon 1:12). Pretty romantic imagery.

Later, the bridegroom lavishly describes the scents of nard and saffron which emanated from his bride (Song of Solomon 4:11–14).

The love this woman demonstrated at Simon's feast was a costly risk, economically and socially, but she concentrated on the only One in the room who mattered to her. Jesus who forgives sins. Jesus who heals diseases. Jesus who announces the kingdom of God. She probably wasn't trying to be significant but was simply expressing her devotion to Jesus.

This was a wildly intimate moment that created discomfort in Simon and the guests as she anointed Jesus's head with oil. It's fair to imagine they were familiar with the poetry of Solomon's love story. Did the references spring to mind, increasing their unease?

The disciples challenged the woman. "Why this waste?" (Matthew 26:8). These men appreciated the value of the oil. They knew of Jesus's love for the disadvantaged, so they scolded her. "This could have been sold for a large sum and given to the poor" (v. 9).

Jesus scolded them back. Of course, care for the poor. Care for the poor whenever you like. They will always be with you. But, He explained, He would not always be with them. This woman had, in her devotion, anointed Him for His burial. "Truly, I say to you, wherever this gospel is proclaimed in the whole world, what she has done will also be told in memory of her" (v. 13).

Her demonstration of love not only ministered to Jesus but also unintentionally exposed the hearts of others. She didn't preach a sermon. She simply acted on her love without concern about who was watching, and her love became a searchlight that revealed the shadows lurking in their hearts.

Her choice to publicly express her love for Jesus without shame or self-concern remains a beacon for us, shining across cultures and years. This woman showed us that the path to a lasting impact for Jesus begins with single-minded attention to and love for Him.

The actual reach of our witness is, like hers, often hidden from our sight. For while some are called to global ministries, many more of us are called to a more local influence. Like the Israelites rebuilding Jerusalem's wall in Nehemiah's day, we too are asked to guard and build our own small section of the "gospel wall" in God's kingdom. We are divinely appointed to humble days, small scopes, and the mystery of God at work in the ordinary.

> **We are divinely appointed to humble days, small scopes, and the mystery of God at work in the ordinary.**

In God's kingdom, it's not only those who accomplish "great things" that have a powerful influence for Christ. It is also those who contribute their widow's mite of devotion, who open their single alabaster jar out of love for Jesus, teaching children, visiting the lonely, building sets for Christmas plays, planting trees, or generously supporting ministries to people they may never meet on earth.

What we see about having a graceful influence from the woman with the alabaster jar is fourfold.

First, graceful influence begins with forgetting ourselves and focusing on Jesus. The devoted woman risked the disapproval and rejection of those gathered to demonstrate her love for Jesus.

Second, influence for God isn't limited by gender. From the opening of Scripture to the close, God demonstrates that men and women have equal opportunity. Both can sin in ways that have lasting negative effects. And both have equal opportunity for redemption in Christ and inclusion in the work of proclaiming His kingdom until He comes. The Holy Spirit is the power behind our lives, and He is not limited by anything about us—not our ethnicity, economic status, appearance, gender, worldly status, or age.

Third, graceful influence involves doing what we *can* do for Him, not what we can't. This woman offered Jesus what she had. She probably wasn't trying to do something that would become a story told to every generation to come. She just expressed love the way she knew how to express it, pouring out what she valued most onto the One she valued above all. We all have unique gifts and ways of expressing ourselves. This variety was God's design so we can lean into Him in love.

Finally, it's God who determines the scope of our influence. No one in that room appeared terribly impressed with what this woman had done. In fact, because her giving illuminated the selfishness of their lives, they probably wished she'd kept her gift to herself. I'm guessing they didn't want this story recorded.

Jesus is the one who determined this would be a story told through the generations. He is also the one who determines the impact of our lives, our stories. When Jesus is central, our ministry can be as far-reaching as a powerful fragrance released from its broken container.

We are, after all, the aroma of Christ. "But thanks be to God, who in Christ always leads us in triumphal procession, and through us spreads the fragrance of the knowledge of him everywhere. For we are the aroma of Christ to God among those who are being saved and among those who are perishing, to one a fragrance from death to death, to the other a fragrance from life to life. Who is sufficient for these things?" (2 Corinthians 2:14–16).

In life, as in that room, our love poured out for Jesus will be a sweet aroma to those open to Jesus's love, but an unpleasant odor to those resisting the repentance to which He calls us. As our lives, out of love for Jesus, are broken and poured out for Him, we become the precious nard that is the aroma of Christ.

The lasting effect of this aroma will be life for all who are being saved.

BIBLE

This woman's story is told in Matthew 26:6–13 and Mark 14:3–9. There are two other stories of Jesus being anointed with oil by a woman. These are found in Luke 7:36–50 and John 12:1–8. What are your thoughts on why there is a similar story told in each of the four gospels? How are they alike? What differences do you see?

Jesus told His followers that loving God and loving others are the greatest commandments (Mark 12:29–31). In what ways do you love God "with all your heart and with all your soul and with all your mind and with all your strength" (v. 30)?

Bible Extra

Read Psalm 23 and consider what significance it may have held for Jesus as His head was anointed with oil in the presence of Judas. Consider how a scent lingers. How powerful is it to imagine that a simple decision you make can linger with others and continue influencing them long after you've left their company.

BATTLE

Not everyone who came to hear Jesus (either in these stories or in other gospel stories) was interested in Him because they loved Him. The woman with the alabaster jar appeared to love Him, but others came to hear Jesus for a variety of reasons. Some hoped He would lead His people to overthrow Rome and save them from oppression (John 6:15). Others wanted to be fed (John 6:26). Some came to argue or scrutinize because He was challenging the current order of their society (Matthew 21:15). Still others probably had not made up their minds about who

Jesus was and what they wanted from Him (Matthew 16:13–16). This is still our battle today.

Have we come to Jesus for Jesus? Do we recognize Him as God and long to focus attention on Him? Or are we there for what we get out of being associated with Him, hoping He'll enrich or empower us?

What made the difference between being the woman with graceful influence through her love versus being one of those scolded by Jesus? How easy is it to behave more like the people reacting indignantly to the woman than like the woman herself? What steps can we take to keep our focus and attention on Jesus? Consider Hebrews 12:1–3 in forming your answer.

Bottom Line

When Jesus is our focus, our ministry
can be like a fragrance released from its
jar that can no longer be contained.

Eve and Mary, the Mother of Jesus

The Impact of Obedience

*For I do not do the good I want, but the evil
I do not want is what I keep on doing.*

Romans 7:19

When Carly moved out of her family home, she had one guiding rule she knew would guarantee success. In every decision, she asked herself what choice her mother would have made—and she did the opposite.

Her mother focused life on her career. Carly became a stay-at-home mom. Her mother divorced two husbands. Carly made sure she and her husband attended a yearly marriage conference. Her mother had no female friends, considering them all competition. Carly developed deep, collaborative friendships with other women. Carly was so certain of her guiding rule that she even made sure to choose a different toothpaste from the one her mother had provided.

Imagine Carly's shock when she was correcting one of her

children one day and, like many of us do, heard her mother's voice come out of her own mouth!

No matter how determined we are not to be like our parents—whether because they made wrong decisions or because we simply want to distinguish ourselves from them—we usually find it's a more challenging goal than we imagined. So even though generations lie between us and the first mother, Eve, she continues to have a powerful and lasting impact.

I catch glimpses of Eve in my mirror all the time. I believe Carly does too.

Of course, initially we're quick to classify Mother Eve's influence as devastatingly negative. But because of God's mercy, that's not Eve's whole story. God allowed her a part in our road to redemption.

Many of us know Eve's story like we know the way home. God created Adam and provided him residence in the lavish garden of Eden, resplendent with trees of every kind. God gave him freedom to eat from all of them except one. God warned him that if he ate from the Tree of the Knowledge of Good and Evil, he would die.

Even though Adam had an easy relationship with God, God decided it wasn't good that Adam was alone. He needed a companion of his own kind. So, from Adam's rib, God formed a woman. She and Adam became one flesh. They were naked and unashamed. It was all so good.

Until, that is, the serpent tempted Eve into doubting both God's goodness and the specific parameters of God's command. Eve chose to disobey God's one restriction, and Adam followed suit. The lasting impact of her—their—disobedience imparted sin, like a virus, throughout all humanity and caused the fall that ruined the entire creation. Death entered the world, casting its long, dark shadow over our lives.

Eve and Adam were ejected from the garden to prevent them from eating from the Tree of Life and living on, trapped in sin.

Because of God's great mercy, however, that is not the final word on Eve's legacy.

We may be justifiably angry with her, this long-past ancestor of ours, for making this terrible choice, but I imagine all of us have done something that caused pain, sadness, or ruin. We've broken an heirloom, a confidence, or a heart. We've done wrong that brought death into a moment, a holiday, or a relationship. We wouldn't want to remain locked forever in that moment.

Imagine Eve's pain for causing the ruin of creation. One hint we have that she took it hard is her name change. Initially, Adam called her Woman, but once they were cursed, Adam called her Eve, meaning "life giving" or "life bearer." Perhaps he thought to give Eve this small comfort. Her actions brought sin and death into the world, but mercifully, God would use her also to bear life.

God didn't end Adam and Eve's lives in the immediate aftermath of their sin. Their choice was terrible and the consequences far-reaching, and yet God wasn't done with either of them. He loved them, after all.

The serpent, Eve, and Adam each received an immediate consequence from God. The serpent was cursed to crawl on his belly (Genesis 3:14); God told Eve her pain would be multiplied in childbearing (v. 16); and Adam's work would be hard, requiring sweat to produce any benefit from his efforts (vv. 17–19).

That God would allow Eve (and Adam) a part in His plan of redemption is hinted in His words to the serpent: "I will put enmity between you and the woman, and between your offspring and her offspring; he shall bruise your head, and you shall bruise his heel" (v. 15).

The theological term for this verse is the *protoevangelium*, the "first gospel." Humanity is cursed because of the fall, but almost immediately God delivers the first promise of redemption to come through a future child. Eve will be the "mother of all living" (v. 20), and one of her descendants will be the promised

Deliverer. This promise is a mercy to Adam and Eve and, indeed, mercy for all of us affected by sin.

Generations later, a young Israelite woman betrothed to a carpenter in Nazareth received what would be to any of us a distressing visitation. While we can certainly see ourselves in Eve, most would be hard-pressed to relate to this teenage virgin face-to-face with the angel Gabriel. Imagine, for a moment, what it was like for her to learn she had the Lord's favor. To learn she would bear a child. To learn this child would be God's Son, the long-awaited Messiah. And after all that, to ask only how it would occur. Mary was a unique and singular woman.

Imagine her poised on the edge of a life she'd anticipated since childhood, then suddenly hearing it was all about to become dramatically different—and yet responding, essentially, with, "Let it be." Let that sink in.

Mary was a woman like us, with the echo of Eve in her bones. But here she was, responding to God with the yes of obedience, resisting the temptation to escape into the life she'd planned. Human, yes. Imperfect and sinful, yes. But obedient in the moment that mattered.

> **Mary was a woman like us, with the echo of Eve in her bones.**

And here is where God's mercy merges Mary's story with Eve's. Eve, who had been *disobedient* in the moment that mattered. Eve, who made the mistake of hearing the serpent out. Eve, who wouldn't rest in the contentment of every tree, save one. Eve, who bit the bait hooking humanity on Satan's hollow promise of fulfillment through following our own way—away from God.

And yet, Eve on whom God had mercy.

God didn't demand Eve's life in the moment of the fall. He didn't destroy her and create a new woman for Adam. He allowed them both to live, albeit not the blissful life He'd planned for them. Instead, a future of frustrating work, pain, and struggle—the life they chose for themselves through disobedience.

We too must sometimes live with the consequences of our sin even after we've repented and received God's forgiveness. But we love a merciful God, and He promises that "for those who love God all things work together for good" (Romans 8:28). Ejection from the garden appears harsh, but it protected Adam and Eve from eating from the Tree of Life and living forever in the consequences of their sin. Sending them away into the rest of the earth was God's initial mercy.

There were further mercies in that God blessed them with children and helped Eve bring them into the world. When, through treachery, Cain killed his brother, Abel, God again had mercy, and Eve bore another son. She named this child Seth, meaning "set in place of."

Eve believed God set this child in place of the one she'd lost, and Seth became the son through whom many believe the bloodline of redemption flowed. Seth's descendants include Noah (Genesis 5). Noah's descendant Shem is in the line of Abraham (Genesis 11). From Abraham came Judah, Jesse, David, and, eventually, Jesus. This lineage is sometimes referred to as "the godly line of Seth," not because every man and woman in that line lived perfect lives but because they placed their faith in God.

Jesus, who obeyed God perfectly, would come from the line of Seth, who was born of Eve, who disobeyed: Jesus, born of obedient Mary, descendant of disobedient Eve.

Mary is a wonderful role model to us because of her obedience to God. Once, a woman from the crowd cried out to Jesus, "Blessed is the womb that bore you, and the breasts at which you nursed!" (Luke 11:27). Jesus replied, "Blessed rather are those who hear the word of God and keep it!" (v. 28).

Jesus praised Mary's obedience. Again, the Bible is full of sinful people in need of a Savior. Mary chose obedience—and blessed are all who do.

Obedience isn't the guarantee of an easy life; Mary experienced much earthly suffering because of her obedience. But she was also privileged to see the risen Redeemer and to be present at the birth of the church, along with other men and women who followed Jesus in the coming of His Holy Spirit (Acts 2).

Sin entered the world through a woman, but so did the One by whom redemption would come. Mary's graceful influence is redemptive. And though Eve's disobedience certainly had far-reaching consequences, God allowed her to also have a part, as the "mother of all living," in His plan of redemption, demonstrating the tenacity of His love and mercy over all creation from beginning to end.

BIBLE

We find Eve's story in Genesis 1–4. One telling of Mary's story is in Luke 1–2. What application do their stories of obedience (or disobedience) have for yours? How do you relate to each woman? How are you like or unlike each one? What does God's mercy on Eve tell you about His character (Exodus 34:6)? What do Mary's struggles as Jesus's mother tell you about the possible personal impact of obedience?

Bible Extra

Read Romans 5:15–18. Whose obedience brought about justification and life? What change has that made in you?

BATTLE

We all struggle with obedience, and we experience sorrow over the consequences of our disobedience. "For I do not do the good I want, but the evil I do not want is what I keep on doing" (Romans 7:19). This ongoing battle is central to most of our lives, but by grace, when we follow Jesus, we have the power of the Holy Spirit to free us to take the godly path.

When have you experienced the power of Jesus to help you obey at a time when you were tempted to go the wrong way? How did this encourage you for future obedience? What difference can it make for you to consider the generational consequences Eve's and Mary's decisions had?

Bottom Line

God's redemptive mercy provides the power
we need to choose obedience that can
ripple through countless generations.

Deborah and Queen Jezebel

The Impact of Godly Influence

Now Deborah, a prophetess, the wife of Lappidoth, was judging Israel at that time. She used to sit under the palm of Deborah between Ramah and Bethel in the hill country of Ephraim, and the people of Israel came up to her for judgment.

Judges 4:4–5

Women influence the world.

Women influence others at home, work, church, missions, military, politics, culture, and through global activism. We influence through formal and informal roles—mothering, marriage, mentoring, ministry, and media. We may influence through serving as queen, through raising the next generation, or by being the woman in the next cubicle, pew, or voting booth, but one way or another, our effect spreads far beyond what we see.

You may not consider yourself an influencer of culture, but you are. You sway the culture in your household or living situation. You contribute to the culture of your friendships, congregation, and community. Are you a hope-filled, positive, affirming contribution or a critical, bitter, sad one?

You may be very aware of your role and your effect. As a leader, you may also impact others in leadership. Some of you have ministries that extend around the globe. The question is, when others walk away from a brush with you, do they walk away uplifted, inspired, and challenged or more susceptible to fear, sadness, worry, or despair?

If we open our eyes to what is unseen, we recognize that through our lives, we all influence others either for Christ or away from Him.

That was the case with two Old Testament women with very different contributions over the course of Israel's history. One woman used her power to inspire others to godly action; the other used hers to draw people to false gods. One, a leader, inspired a Jewish military general and his commanders, who had grown soft. The other, a queen, enabled a selfish king to further indulge himself at the expense of those who relied on him.

Deborah was the fourth judge of Israel, a wife, and a prophetess. Scripture records that she sat beneath a palm tree, where people came to her for wisdom. Many major biblical figures are associated with trees or plants. Noah had his olive branch from an olive tree. Abraham sat beneath the oaks at Mamre. Moses heard God speak from the burning bush. Elijah lay down under a broom tree in his discouragement. God taught Jonah a lesson through a vine. The palm is associated with victory, and that's what the Israelites experienced under Deborah's leadership.

Palms can be metaphors for righteousness, and we know Deborah's judgments were righteous. They are symbolic of flourishing in challenging conditions, just as Deborah flourished despite challenging responsibilities. Palms can flex under much weight and not break. Deborah yielded in agreeing to go to battle to support Barak, and she didn't break, despite the demands of battle. Her style of leadership was an oasis of strength in a desert barren of fortitude from the other leaders of Israel during her times (Judges 4:6–9; 5:6–7).

Deborah received word from the Lord for the military leader, Barak. God would give the armies of Sisera into his hands. Barak agreed to go to battle only if Deborah would go with him. She consented but warned him that he would not receive the glory for Sisera's defeat. That would go to Jael, the wife of a Kenite, who lured Sisera into her tent and drove a tent peg through his temple.

Their victory led to forty years of rest in their land. Deborah and Barak celebrated with a song that captures the influence of a significantly unique perspective on the military endeavor. "I, Deborah, arose as a mother in Israel" (Judges 5:7). As "mother" to her people, she shared credit by celebrating Jael's part in the victory, and she mentioned the grief of Sisera's mother, highlighting both the glory and the often-overlooked cost of war at home.

Deborah described their times as so dangerous that people no longer traveled on the public roads. The warriors were soft. Few were willing to take up sword and shield to defend the people until Deborah arose and inspired them to act. "My heart goes out to the commanders of Israel who offered themselves willingly," she said, commending those who found the courage to defend their people (Judges 5:9).

Deborah was a protective, inspirational, God-confident influencer who called out those who had been looking the other way. She entered battle for the defenseless and rejoiced in her victory while maintaining sensitivity toward the human cost. In her brief story, we see an influential leader comfortable in her gifts, calling, and decisions, partnered with other leaders, unafraid to battle, creative and celebratory in the day of victory.

Deborah's impact stretched at least through the next four decades of rest, but she continues to inspire people today. Modern Christians look to her example of strength, wisdom, courage, and collaboration to inform their own leadership. Her partnership with Barak was a benefit to him and to Israel. Because of her example, he chose faith in God's leadership, and he wisely trusted her gifts.

Conversely, Jezebel demonstrated the worst kind of influence. Where Deborah inspired those around her and appealed to their greater qualities, Jezebel indulged and exploited the worst of her royal husband's tendencies while inciting fear and idol worship in the people they led. Deborah sought the voice of the Lord and was unafraid to proclaim God's message; Jezebel despised and murdered the prophets of God, seeking to silence His voice in her times.

Jezebel's husband, King Ahab, was an Israelite, but he was an evil king, "more than all who were before him" (1 Kings 16:30). Ahab went against God's directions, marrying outside the faith and pursuing idolatry (Deuteronomy 7:3–4; 1 Kings 16:31).

Considering the circumstances, we wouldn't necessarily expect Jezebel to make godly choices. Other Gentiles living amongst the Jewish people had chosen to follow their God. Jezebel, on the other hand, doesn't even tolerate the religion of her new people; rather, she defies God and seeks to destroy His prophets. Filled with religious zeal for an idol, not the Living God, Jezebel is the embodiment of Romans 10:3: "Being ignorant of the righteousness of God, and seeking to establish their own, they did not submit to God's righteousness." Understanding the context in which she made her decisions, we can still observe and learn from their outcomes.

These were the days of the prophet Elijah. The presence of the prophets of Baal and the Asherah poles in God's land—Jezebel's doing—were abhorrent to God. Elijah had a great showdown with these false prophets and prevailed. When Jezebel heard this, she threatened to kill Elijah, as she had many other prophets of God.

The fruit of Jezebel and Ahab's reign was mass executions and an escalation of idolatry that would plague Israel for decades to come. They were a well-matched pair, united in evil plans.

Since Ahab joined Jezebel in the worship of Baal, Jezebel would have had little incentive to change. Still, she had ears like every other person in the land who heard the prophets. She knew the outcome of Elijah's showdown with the prophets of Baal. She was free to change. She chose destruction and used her power to serve her own needs, not those of her people.

Ahab was not only rebellious; he was also greedy and small. He envied his neighbor Naboth's diminutive plot of land and tried to buy it, but Naboth declined, wanting to preserve his inheritance. When Ahab pouted (1 Kings 21), Jezebel didn't encourage him to be satisfied with all he already had but, instead, fueled his craving for more. "There was none who sold himself to do what was evil in the sight of the LORD like Ahab, whom Jezebel his wife incited" (1 Kings 21:25). Jezebel devised a plot against Naboth, inciting the local leaders against him. She orchestrated Naboth's stoning on false charges so that Ahab was free to take his land. But God, through Elijah, proclaimed that for his sins, disaster would come upon Ahab, and Jezebel would be eaten by dogs.

Ahab initially repented in response to Elijah's message, delaying his punishment for a time. Jezebel had the same opportunity to repent or at least support Ahab's change of heart. She did not.

> **God created the world, and there is a way it works, even for people who don't acknowledge His existence.**

Jezebel's legacy is one of fear, deception, idolatry, and murder. Her name has become a watchword for such. It wasn't easy for the succeeding king and those who followed him to undo her damage. There was much bloodshed in ridding the land of the worship of false gods. That spiritual adultery lingered to poison Israel for decades. God created the world, and there is a way it works, even for people who don't acknowledge His existence.

God sees our choices and the ways our actions affect others. Deborah's godly influence, He rewarded with victory. Jezebel's ungodly influence led to her demise. Each woman continues to instruct—one as a guiding light, the other as a caution.

BIBLE

Deborah's story is in Judges 4 and 5. She was a leader influencing other leaders. What has been your influence on leaders (or coleaders) who needed encouragement to do what is right? What do you see as the hallmark traits of Deborah's unique style? Look especially at her victory song and note the imagery. Where do you see the influence of her perspective in that song?

God warns the kings of Israel against marrying foreign women in 1 Kings 11:1–2 and Deuteronomy 7:3. How does the story of Jezebel's sway over Ahab illustrate the wisdom of God's command? Both stories illustrate the way we affect those partnered with us both in marriage and in leadership. What lesson can we apply to our relationships in business, ministry, and personal life?

Bible Extra

Jezebel's story is recorded in 1 Kings 18–19. Read Revelation 2:18–29. What could have been the effect on John's Jewish readers of hearing a woman referred to as "Jezebel"?

BATTLE

We often lament our perceived lack of influence. Yet when we see one of our negative traits appearing in our children or watch as our bad mood infects a small group meeting, we're suddenly confronted with the power we actually yield, too often without even thinking.

God doesn't expect perfection from us, but we must believe Him and trust that our choices matter—both great and small.

Consider the women who have influenced you toward God. Were they perfect? Well known? Polished in every way? What form did their influence take? What are the opportunities in your life right now to impact others? Write a description of the type of influence you want to have and ask God to help you be that person in the name of Jesus.

Bottom Line

The influence of one person can turn
the tide of a family, church, business,
community, or even nation toward God.

Abigail and Sapphira

The Impact of Discretion

Discretion will watch over you, understanding will guard you.
Proverbs 2:11

Two marriages. Difficult men. Different wives. Distinct choices.

We've all seen challenging marriages. Mismatched couples sometimes leave us wondering how they ever got together. Any binding relationship, whether marriage, family, friendship, organization, or business, can get complicated. We find ourselves in situations where we have to choose between doing what is right and keeping the relationship intact.

In biblical times, most marriages were arranged, so it's likely that neither of the women we'll consider in this chapter had much say in who her partner would be. We don't know for certain, but that was the culture.

That didn't, however, leave these women without agency. In Proverbs 31, King Lemuel describes a godly woman who managed her household, ran a business, and exercised great independence in her activities. Within their marriages, Abigail and Sapphira illustrate that even in complicated circumstances we can employ either wise or devious decision-making. One woman chose discretion and gained honor; the other chose device and paid the ultimate price.

Contronyms are single words that can mean opposite things. For example, the word *cleave*: you can cleave a watermelon in two, but you can also cleave to another person. Or *dust*: you can dust a donut with powdered sugar, but when you dust the tabletop the donut sat on, you're clearing away the sugar, not adding it. The Hebrew word *mᵉzimmâ*, translated "discretion," is a contronym. It can mean "purpose," such as a good, wise plan; or it can mean "device or plot," as in an evil plan.[2] *Discretion* in English can mean "to exercise good judgment," but sometimes people are asked to be *discreet* by keeping quiet about evil deeds. The dual nature of this word serves our understanding of these two women.

Abigail and Sapphira. Women of different times and different Testaments, and yet they shared similar qualities and situations. Both had shrewd judgment and were quick to take the measure of a situation. Both were faced with answering for family decisions. Abigail was surprised by the one her harsh husband made. Sapphira knew of her husband's bad decision and appears to have at least consented to a cover-up. Each woman had to be quick-witted in high-stakes circumstances, and each had agency to make a godly choice even when her partner did not.

Abigail's story in 1 Samuel 25 occurs just after Samuel died. David was running from King Saul. He and his men roamed the borderlands of Israel. As they did, they protected shepherds in the hills. This was a common courtesy, but David probably also remembered his days as a shepherd and was inclined to care for others entrusted to be alone with their flocks. Specifically, in this story, David's men had protected the shepherds of a wealthy Calebite, Nabal, whom the Bible describes as "harsh and badly behaved" (1 Samuel 25:3).

At shearing season, David's men rightly anticipated an invitation to Nabal's celebration feast in gratitude for their protection.

But their request to be included received a rude reply. Nabal denied any responsibility to repay the favor, and David, responding impulsively to the offense, ordered his men to teach Nabal a lesson.

Fortunately for all who worked under Nabal, one of the shepherds reported to Abigail what happened. He concluded, "Now therefore know this and consider what you should do, for harm is determined against our master and against all his house, and he is such a worthless man that one cannot speak to him" (v. 17). Imagine the desperation of these family men, knowing that Nabal's brutish manner put them all at risk of death.

Abigail was "discerning and beautiful" (v. 3). In the moment of decision, she exercised her discernment and devised a plan God used to rescue her household.

Abigail gathered enough food and wine for David's men (six hundred or so) and loaded it on donkeys. She sent her servant ahead of her with the provisions, and when she reached David, she fell to the ground before him and appealed for mercy.

> **In her actions and speech, Abigail showed keen understanding of the politics of the times, the power of God, and what motivates godly men.**

Abigail asked for his pardon. She admitted her husband was a fool (which is what the name Nabal means), and she explained that, regrettably, she, as woman of the household, had not seen the men David sent with his request. She offered blessings for David's future and wisely appealed to David's reliance on his God. Every decision she made demonstrated wisdom, intelligence, and discretion.

In her actions and speech, Abigail showed keen understanding of the politics of the times, the power of God, and what motivates godly men. And although she was frank that her husband's foolish actions were responsible for the situation, yet she honored him by assuming responsibility for the affront. (Of course, David was aware of Nabal's culpability.)

David was rightly impressed and deeply grateful. He praised Abigail's discretion and blessed her for preventing bloodshed. How grateful the families of the men working for her husband must have been that day! Her actions averted certain death for the entire household.

Nabal by this time was hosting a feast and full of wine. So Abigail, returning home, again used her discretion and waited until he was sober before informing him of her actions. When Nabal finally understood what had occurred, "his heart died within him" (v. 37). Ten days later, God ended Nabal's life. When David heard, he knew God had avenged him. And so impressed was he with Abigail that he sent for her to be his wife.

Now flash-forward to the New Testament, to another husband-wife duo.

Ananias and Sapphira were present at the birth of the church, recorded in Acts. Chapter 4 tells how God's people willingly sold their possessions, lands, and houses so no one would be in need. The disciple Barnabas sold a field and laid all the proceeds at the apostles' feet. Ananias, perhaps hoping for praise and gratitude similar to what was likely bestowed on Barnabas, also sold a piece of property. However, he decided to secretly keep back some of the proceeds for himself, with the full knowledge of his wife.

Now, it would have been his right to retain a portion. The problem lay in his dishonesty. Ananias lied that he was giving the church the full price he obtained for the field. Peter reprimanded him for lying to the Holy Spirit, and Ananias died at Peter's feet.

Three hours later, Sapphira arrived, unaware of her husband's fate. Peter asked Sapphira if the price donated to the church was the full price the couple received for the land.

Here was her moment. Ananias wasn't present. Sapphira had freedom. She could have chosen truth. Instead, she stuck by her device, to be discreet about the evil decision. She lied just as her husband had lied, telling Peter they had donated the full amount of their land sale.

Immediately, Sapphira paid the same price as Ananias for lying to the Holy Spirit—death by her own devices.

Sapphira's story ends tragically here. The effect of her behavior was fear, spread to all who heard what happened. Such is the legacy of those who choose complicity with evil plots and devices—sadness and fear.

Abigail's story continued. She lived as one of King David's wives, and 1 Chronicles 3:1 says she bore him a son named Daniel, meaning "God is my judge." Her discretion not only averted the deaths of many in her household, but it prevented David from falling prey to his own rash judgment. Abigail prophesied that God would make David a "sure house" (1 Samuel 25:28), meaning an established lineage. Certainly, this moment was a strong reminder to David to leave vengeance with the Lord.

Abigail continues to inspire intelligent, beautiful women cornered in difficult circumstances, reminding us that we still have choices. We can reject devices that lead to death and instead exercise discretion that leads to life.

BIBLE

What are your thoughts about Sapphira's story? Honestly, it's a hard story to process. Why would God act so swiftly to punish deception against the Holy Spirit from within the new church?

Abigail's story is recorded in 1 Samuel 25. Read Abigail's appeal to David in verses 28 through 31, and consider the wisdom and discretion demonstrated in her words. Why do you believe this made such an impression on the king?

Bible Extra

Proverbs 11:22 reads, "Like a gold ring in a pig's snout is a beautiful woman without discretion." Write a paraphrase of that proverb with an updated image for our times.

God didn't punish Ananias and Sapphira for withholding part of their proceeds but for lying about what they had given. Second Corinthians 9:6–8 makes clear we're not expected to give "under compulsion" or "reluctantly." We give out of gratitude for all God has done.

BATTLE

We all face difficult moments where doing the right thing will cost us something. When someone close to us takes a sinful path, we can sin by joining them or by agreeing to cover for them. Choosing to take a godly path opposed to theirs is very difficult. It's a good argument for making careful decisions about our most intimate alliances, but sometimes people in our inner circle present us with terrible dilemmas, and we can feel trapped.

In *Man's Search for Meaning*, Viktor Frankl, a Nazi concentration camp survivor, writes, "Everything can be taken from a man but one thing: the last of the human freedoms—to choose one's attitude in any given set of circumstances, to choose one's own way."[3] Discretion must be developed day by day. It doesn't just appear in the moment of hard decision. How will you move toward developing it today?

Bottom Line

Godly discretion guides us when we must
make the costly choice to do the right thing.

5

Delilah and Ruth

The Impact of Devotion

*The women said to Naomi, "Blessed be the LORD,
who has not left you this day without a redeemer, and
may his name be renowned in Israel! He shall be to
you a restorer of life and a nourisher of your old age,
for your daughter-in-law who loves you, who is more
to you than seven sons, has given birth to him."*

Ruth 4:14–15

Delilah was a woman who apparently knew how to watch out for herself.

She lived in Sorek, which was the borderland between the Israelites and their enemies, the Philistines. *Delilah* is Hebrew and means "feeble, delicate, or weak." In contrast, she was loved by Samson, a Nazarite renowned for his strength.

By the time we encounter Delilah, we've already witnessed many of Samson's feats of strength, but we also know he has played the field with women. He'd married and lost one Philistine, and just before he encountered Delilah, he visited a prostitute. Samson had a special calling, but he often acted selfishly and impulsively. He used his strength not only to protect his people but also to exact personal revenge. Historically, he's a hero of Israel, but morally, he's no role model.

Perhaps Samson's reputation had preceded him, and Delilah assessed their relationship as an opportunity. The Philistine leaders saw a strength in Samson they couldn't explain or imagine defeating. When they approached Delilah with a potentially lucrative offer, she demonstrated her devotion to self and agreed to accept money in exchange for revealing the secret of Samson's strength.

Delilah was surrounded by people largely devoted to themselves, even Samson. Throughout the repeated cycles of sin detailed in Judges, the Israelites had chosen devotion to their own interests or to idols over devotion to God's ways. Because Israel consistently did what was evil in God's sight, He had given them over to the Philistines for forty years (Judges 13:1).

Unlike women like Rahab or Ruth, Delilah appears to have been a woman who didn't even attempt to resist the prevailing current of her society. Delilah's devotion to self wasn't unusual then. "Everyone did what was right in his own eyes" (Judges 21:25). Society was a free-for-all. So, to be fair, Delilah may have learned through hard experiences that if she didn't look out for herself, no one else would. Others may even have admired Delilah's shrewd self-protection and independence.

But understanding the context of Delilah's choice doesn't excuse it. Devotion to self leads to corruption, hardness of heart, and loss of both intimacy and community. God's relationship with us isn't transactional but unconditional, and He wants us to love as He does. Sadly, Delilah may not have experienced this relationship with the God of Israel, especially when much of Israel was making poor decisions too. This is why those who represent God must represent Him accurately. People are hungry for a God who loves, and our lives can point the way to Him. Still, while Delilah's decision occurred in a sea of wrong decisions, she could have chosen differently.

Delilah persisted with Samson four times to get him to reveal the secret to his strength. Three times, he lied. Then, the fourth time, even when the evidence was clear that she'd conspired with his enemies, he revealed the truth. (Go figure.) The Bible says that "he told her all his heart" (Judges 16:17). Up to this point, she knew he'd been playing her. She asked for the truth; he delivered lies. But this time, not only did he tell her his heart, but she knew it (v. 18).

People are hungry for a God who loves, and our lives can point the way to Him.

If this were a modern movie, Samson's choice to be vulnerable would have melted her heart. Delilah had an opportunity here to take a different way. She could have taken one step toward devotion to another person. Sadly, this isn't a feature film but history. Delilah chose to remain consistent with her former choices, as Samson could have reasonably anticipated. She sold him out.

While he slept, she had a man shave Samson's head. When the Philistines arrived, his strength was gone. They blinded him, bound him, and imprisoned him. God records one clue that He wasn't done with His plan for Samson in verse 22: "The hair of his head began to grow again after it had been shaved."

In her devotion to self, Delilah opted for the immediate reward of riches. Israel was left without a judge and protector all the while Samson's hair grew. That took time, so although Samson did eventually deliver Israel, their oppression was extended. True to her name, Delilah brought weakness to Samson and enfeebled the defenses of the Israelites.

We never hear more about her.

There is another woman from those times, living surrounded by people devoted to themselves. The Bible allows us a close-up of her family who lived "in the days when the judges ruled"

(Ruth 1:1). Not only were these people largely self-serving, but they had to survive a famine. Hunger doesn't bring out the best in people but instead exposes the worst.

Ruth's mother-in-law, Naomi, and Naomi's husband and sons were Israelites who moved to Moab during the food shortage. Ruth herself was a Moabitess. The Moabites were descended from Abraham's nephew, Lot, but they were an idolatrous tribe. Naomi's sons married Moabite women, Orpah and Ruth, but by the close of a decade, all three women were widowed.

Naomi was embittered by all she'd suffered and lost. Hearing there was food once again in Israel, she decided to go home, but released her daughters-in-law to return to their people and find husbands among their own tribesmen.

Orpah agreed to leave, but Ruth expressed unusual devotion to Naomi and to God. "Do not urge me to leave you or to return from following you. For where you go I will go, and where you lodge I will lodge. Your people shall be my people, and your God my God. Where you die I will die, and there will I be buried. May the LORD do so to me and more also if anything but death parts me from you" (Ruth 1:16–17).

Word of Ruth's uncommon faithfulness spread among the Israelites. Her devotion to Naomi above herself impressed a relative of Naomi's named Boaz, described as a worthy man—someone who, like Ruth, was not devoted solely to self.

Boaz blessed Ruth, "The LORD repay you for what you have done, and a full reward be given you by the LORD, the God of Israel, under whose wings you have come to take refuge" (Ruth 2:12). He encouraged her to glean in his field under his protection.

Eventually, Boaz became Ruth's "kinsman-redeemer," the relation who agreed to marry her and care for both her and Naomi. Their relationship is a foreshadowing of our redemption in Christ. Their firstborn son, Obed, is listed in the genealogy of Jesus. Ruth is one of only five women listed in Matthew 1. Her son Obed is David's grandfather.

The lasting influence of Ruth's devotion is this beautiful story of redemption.

Our culture has elevated the romantic love of marriage, but in ancient biblical culture, marriage was a practical necessity, especially for women. While some sentimentalize Ruth and Boaz—and who's to say they didn't find love?—this is nevertheless a story of survival.

Naomi's loss of her husband and sons meant she was plunged into poverty. Ruth may have had opportunity to find shelter with her birth family or a new husband had she followed Orpah in returning home. Instead, she joined Naomi in her impoverished situation.

Ruth humbled herself to participate in gleaning among a people who were foreign to her and to offer herself for redemption to Boaz, a much older man (Ruth 3:10). She left all that was familiar to go to her mother-in-law's people, even committing to follow their God.

Just as Ruth was entirely dependent on finding a kinsman-redeemer, so are we, in our sin. Sin has left us impoverished of soul, but Jesus has given His life to redeem us. There was new life on the other side of Ruth's redemption, and there is an even greater new life through our redemption in Christ.

Ruth demonstrated that even when everyone around us chooses devotion to self, we can be devoted to a greater story. That decision will lead us to others also choosing against the grain, and together, we create a counterculture that represents God in our times.

BIBLE

Read 1 Timothy 4:1 and 2 Timothy 3:1–4. How are people "in later times" or "in the last days" described? What does this reveal about their devotion? Is it to self or to God? In contrast, where are the devotions of Christians to lie? Read Ephesians 4:2; Romans 12:10–12; and 1 Kings 8:61. How does it stand out in our generation when an individual or group of people demonstrates love for others over self?

Bible Extra

There are women who are only mentioned in Scripture, with no details of their stories, but it's likely a tribute to their devotion to Jesus and to others. Both Mary the wife of Clopas and Mary the mother of James and Joses are noted around Jesus's burial and resurrection. They were devoted disciples. Paul sends greetings from, among others, Claudia, from his imprisonment in Rome (2 Timothy 4:21). She was also a devoted follower of Jesus and worked alongside Paul.

BATTLE

Never underestimate the force of the prevailing culture on our spirits. As more and more people devote themselves to their own interests, we will face times when, like Delilah, it may appear sensible and safest to follow suit.

This theme of looking out for self above others is also becoming a popular theme in our fiction. One TV series portrays a world where anyone who stands for good or for looking out for others is destroyed, while those who understand that only power rules survive. In this fictional world, devotion to self and transactional relationships are revered. Those who excel at them stand a chance of gaining the iron throne. But that fictional world is without an active God.

Many idols, passions, and desires will tempt us to turn our devotion to things that aren't pleasing to God. God inspired the recording of Ruth's story. We can see that her godly devotion led to blessings for generations. As we consider the lasting influence of our lives, we can trust, even in the face of countless messages to the contrary, that devotion to God will benefit not only us but generations to come.

Bottom Line

When everyone around us is choosing devotion to self, we can devote ourselves to a greater story.

6

Athaliah and Jehosheba

The Impact of Protecting Life

*The wise woman builds her house, but the
foolish pulls it down with her hands.*

Proverbs 14:1 NKJV

Our movie and story culture appears to glamorize or fasci-
nate itself with evil characters. Sometimes it even makes
villains the primary focus. Modern writers have apparently lost the skill of writing about wise or noble characters in
interesting ways.

In real time, most of us find that those who choose evil are
simply not as interesting or deep as those who choose to live
decent, godly lives. Evil dulls a person and reduces him or her
to a caricature of their original design. One evil, brutish, violent
person is very much like the next.

One mark of those who consistently choose evil is that they
are bent on protecting themselves, even sometimes at the cost
of others' lives. In contrast, those who are godly and interesting
place others first and work to protect lives, sometimes at the
expense of their own.

Consider the very positive move most news stations are taking in the wake of incidents of mass violence. Rather than reporting exclusively on the perpetrator, networks now devote more time to talking about the lives of the lost. Instead of recounting another loner who kept to himself or herself before emerging to commit a heinous act, stories focus on hard-working individuals with dreams, unique visions for life, and families, friends, and coworkers who admired them. It is, after all, better to fill the headlines with news of those who choose life over those who choose death.

Let's look at the decisions made by two women engaged in the same biblical story.

Sadly, we only have two verses (in each of two retellings of this story) about the woman who chose life. We have much more material on the one who chose death for others to save herself (2 Kings 11; 2 Chronicles 22). But I'd much prefer to highlight and write the most about Jehosheba.

Jehosheba is the heroine of this chapter in Israel's history. She risked her life to save a child. In protecting one life, Jehosheba saved her nation from a woman so obsessed with preserving her own life that she destroyed many others.

But sadly, to appreciate Jehosheba's heroism, we must first spend a few moments with Athaliah. Her name deserves to be forgotten.

Athaliah was, as we say, "connected." Some Bible translations say she was the granddaughter of King Omri; others say she was his daughter. This would have made her either King Ahab's daughter or his sister. Coming from that household, we can imagine she was at least knowledgeable of the machinations of Queen Jezebel, a Baal-worshiping, self-centered ruler. And would have witnessed the evil actions of at least two kings of Israel who compromised their faith with idolatry. These were not promising influences.

The kingdom was divided with Israel in the north and Judah in the south. Judah was the smaller kingdom, but it retained Jerusalem at its heart. Both kingdoms prospered under godly kings but suffered under evil ones.

Athaliah was the wife of Jehoram, king of Judah. Jehoram's father, Jehoshaphat, is remembered as a good and godly king for most of his reign. Still, he wavered toward the end, resulting in idolatry springing up again in the land. Idol worship had almost been extinguished, but the embers smoldered again under Jehoshaphat.

Those embers reignited with wicked Jehoram's blessing. When he died, Athaliah's son, Ahaziah, ascended to the throne and, under the counsel of his mother, outdid even his father in evil. "He also walked in the ways of the house of Ahab, for his mother was his counselor in doing wickedly" (2 Chronicles 22:3). When Ahaziah was assassinated after less than a year on the throne, Athaliah, clearly unwilling to lose her grip on power, acted on her own behalf.

This next part is almost too terrible to tell. "Now when Athaliah the mother of Ahaziah saw that her son was dead, she arose and destroyed all the royal family" (2 Kings 11:1). This means she killed her own children, her grandchildren, and all offspring of Ahaziah who might be linked to the throne by blood, thereby potentially staking a claim over her. So obsessed was she with maintaining her own power that she was willing to end their line with her reign.

Her plans might have destroyed the kingdom if it weren't for one courageous act captured in two little words—"But Jehosheba" (v. 2).

Jehosheba was Ahaziah's sister and the wife of Jehoiada the priest. She's named as daughter of King Joram (Jehoram) but was not linked by blood to Athaliah. In those times, kings had children by other wives and concubines, so we just don't know who her mother was.

What we do know is that she defied Athaliah.

> But Jehosheba, the daughter of King Joram, sister of Ahaziah, took Joash the son of Ahaziah and stole him away from among the king's sons

who were being put to death, and she put him and his nurse in a bedroom. Thus they hid him from Athaliah, so that he was not put to death. And he remained with her six years, hidden in the house of the LORD, while Athaliah reigned over the land. (2 Kings 11:2–3)

This passage is echoed in the 2 Chronicles 22 version, where Jehosheba is referred to as Jehoshabeath.

In the seventh year of Athaliah's wrongful reign, Jehoiada arranged for Joash to be crowned rightful king, and Athaliah was executed for her crimes. She was the only woman ever to sit on David's throne, but she stole that seat, abused her power, and killed nearly her entire family to secure it. People so obsessed with self will justify causing emotional, mental, physical, or reputational harm to those who obstruct their desires.

Athaliah's choices echo her predecessor Jezebel's. Jezebel's actions rippled through generations; influence, whether for good or evil, can sprout whenever the soil or season allows.

Joash was seven when he became king, and he reigned forty years in Jerusalem (2 Chronicles 24:1–2). While Jehosheba's husband, Jehoiada, lived, Joash did what was right in the eyes of the Lord. Rather than being years of peace and godly prosperity, those years might have been torturous for the Israelites if Jehosheba hadn't risked her life to protect Joash. Her graceful influence provided decades of rightful worship in Jerusalem.

Sadly, when Jehoiada died, Joash was influenced by the deadly root of idolatry that still lingered thanks to Jezebel and Athaliah. But by protecting his life, Jehosheba influenced Israel for good for many, many years prior.

Jehosheba can continue to inspire us today to make decisions that lead to life, even at great inconvenience or risk. Jesus told us He came to bring abundant life (John 10:10), while God's enemy is set on destruction and death. Godly judgments lead to life—the health, growth, and continuation—of relationship, community, and soul (Deuteronomy 30:19–20). Ungodly, self-centered judgments often lead to death of relationship, community, heart, soul, and even body. Godly actions move us toward God; ungodly actions move us away from Him. Athaliah, like Jezebel before her, chose to resolve her problems by taking the lives of others. Her impact was fear and death.

Risking much to save a life is a theme repeated throughout Scripture. The midwives defied Pharaoh (Exodus 1:17). Jochebed put Moses in the river (2:2–3). Pharaoh's daughter drew Moses out (2:5–6). Rahab protected the spies of Israel (Joshua 2:6). When Herod sought to take Jesus's life, Mary and Joseph did what was likely disruptive and inconvenient to keep Him safe (Matthew 2:13–14). Priscilla and Aquila risked their lives to save Paul (Romans 16:3–4).

Harriet Tubman escaped slavery but returned to the South at least thirteen times to free others and guide them along the Underground Railroad. Sir Nicholas Winton, a British stockbroker, saved the lives of over 669 children, most of them Jewish, by arranging their safe passage from Czechoslovakia to England during World War II. Moira Smith, an officer with the New York Police Department, gave her life on 9/11 after helping others escape the building that collapsed on her. Generations exist today because of these individuals' brave acts.

Countless unsung men and women are quietly obeying God's Word and making unselfish decisions to serve their families, communities, businesses, and complete strangers, people who right now are contributing to a culture, to a kingdom of life and light. Sadly, we also hear stories of narcissistic individuals whose selfish ways damage entire generations, congregations, or ministries.

The child whom Jehosheba saved inspired many for good that resonated for generations. There is no telling what lasting damage Athaliah would have inflicted on Israel and on history had her corrupt reign endured beyond her seventh year.

"But Jehosheba" are words that should inspire each of us to choose life always.

BIBLE

Read 2 Kings 11 and 2 Chronicles 22 to see this story for yourself.

Athaliah's decision to kill to secure her situation made sense from her worldview. She valued power and clearly didn't fear God. Perhaps she didn't even believe God existed. Her choices led away from God to death.

> **Choosing life isn't as simple as deciding not to murder or kill.**

Jehosheba's protection of the infant Joash was astonishing and brave—much like the men and women mentioned who risked their own recapture, hid Jewish people from Nazis, or ran into a burning tower. Jehosheba chose life for another, not knowing if it would cost her own life; her focus was toward God on behalf of her people. What inspires people to protect life even as those around them choose harm or even death for others to secure their own wants?

Bible Extra

Read Proverbs 14:27 and 19:23 and Luke 12:4–7. How do these passages shed light on what may have influenced both women?

BATTLE

Choosing death over life comes in many forms. Most of us are probably not tempted to end another person's life, but our actions can lead to smaller deaths. Death of relationship. Death of love. Death of hope. Choosing life isn't as simple as deciding not to murder or kill. We must also be active in contributing to a society that sustains life through nourishing food, shelter, clothing, and safety. And we must concern ourselves with contributing to the eternal life of others by representing the gospel of Jesus.

What actions do you take to support life in your culture and community? How does your understanding of God provide you courage? Do you trust, like Jehosheba, that one person can make a difference that affects many? How does that empower and embolden you?

Bottom Line

"But Jehosheba."

Rebekah and Hannah

The Impact of Prayer

*He told them a parable to the effect that they
ought always to pray and not lose heart.*

Luke 18:1

Rebekah and Hannah, two Old Testament women, had some things in common. Each experienced infertility and each became pregnant in response to prayer—Rebekah's husband Isaac prayed for her, and Hannah prayed on her own. Each gave birth to sons with powerful destinies. Each had to release their sons to God and send them away.

The difference between the two is that Hannah was steadfast in prayer and trusted God with the future while Rebekah engaged manipulation and deceit to secure her son's future. Their choice is one we often wrestle with. Will we try to grasp what we need on our own or invite God through prayer to work in us and for us?

Hannah was married to Elkanah, who had a second wife named Peninnah (1 Samuel 1:1–2). Elkanah would travel to Shiloh yearly to worship and sacrifice to God. He gave a portion of the sacrifice to Peninnah and her children but to Hannah "he gave a double portion, because he loved her, though the Lord had closed her womb" (1 Samuel 1:5).

Peninnah tormented Hannah over her barrenness, especially when they went up for the sacrifice. This weighed on Hannah so much, she would weep and not eat. Elkanah assured her of his love, but nothing fulfilled her longing for a child.

One year, praying in the temple, Hannah promised God that if He gave her a son, she would give him back to the Lord. She wept with such intensity that Eli, the priest, accused her of drunkenness. But Hannah defended herself. "No, my lord, I am a woman troubled in spirit. I have drunk neither wine nor strong drink, but I have been pouring out my soul before the LORD. Do not regard your servant as a worthless woman, for all along I have been speaking out of my great anxiety and vexation" (1 Samuel 1:15–16). Eli then blessed her petition to God.

Have you ever had such a deeply felt need you wept before God in prayer? Have you ever prayed with such intensity that it concerned others? That was the pain and passion Hannah poured out before God.

In response, God remembered Hannah. She gave birth to Samuel. When he was weaned, she returned with Elkanah to Shiloh and presented him at the temple, reminding Eli that she was the woman who prayed, and here was her answer. She released Samuel back to God, trusting Him with the child for which she had longed.

God blessed Hannah with more children (1 Samuel 2:21), and Samuel grew to become a great prophet, guiding both King Saul and King David. Samuel's faith was remarkable, but he was, after all, born of a woman with remarkable faith.

Hannah's legacy, however, isn't only through the work and leadership of her son Samuel. Hannah has been an example of faith and prayer for people throughout the ages of faith. She exemplifies the persistence in prayer Jesus described in a parable.

In a certain city there was a judge who neither
feared God nor respected man. And there was a
widow in that city who kept coming to him and
saying, "Give me justice against my adversary."
For a while he refused, but afterward he said to
himself, "Though I neither fear God nor respect
man, yet because this widow keeps bothering me,
I will give her justice, so that she will not beat me
down by her continual coming." And the Lord
said, "Hear what the unrighteous judge says. And
will not God give justice to his elect, who cry to
him day and night? Will he delay long over them?
I tell you, he will give justice to them speedily.
Nevertheless, when the Son of Man comes, will
he find faith on earth?" (Luke 18:2–8)

Persistence in prayer can be a powerful force, but many of us
give up too quickly. We imagine either God hasn't heard or He
hasn't responded, when really He's urging us to persevere, to
continue to pray, to petition, or to intercede without ceasing.
Prayer isn't inaction any more than meeting with a powerful
world leader to request help is inaction. Pray is often the very
action God wants us to take.

We know little about Hannah other than her faith in God and
her prayer. And we know only a little more about Rebekah.

When Abraham sought a wife for Isaac, he sent his trusted
servant all the way back to his homeland to secure a woman
from his own family. Rebekah was Abraham's great-niece; she
was beautiful and apparently not afraid of hard work. When
Abraham's servant asked her for water, she offered to also provide water for his camels—no light work.

This was the sign the servant had asked of God, so a marriage was arranged. Even though it would require Rebekah to
travel far and leave all she knew, she agreed to become the wife of

Abraham's son. I'm sure it helped knowing Abraham had become prosperous and that Isaac would inherit all his father owned.

Rebekah was barren until "Isaac prayed to the LORD for his wife, because she was barren. And the LORD granted his prayer, and Rebekah his wife conceived" (Genesis 25:21).

The twins Rebekah carried, Esau and Jacob, wrestled with one another in her womb. When she asked God what was going on, He told her she carried within her two great nations, and the older son would serve the younger (v. 23). Rebekah witnessed the power of God answering prayer both in the conception of her sons and in the prophecy about their futures. But somewhere along the way, she decided the rest relied on her. I can relate.

Esau was his father Isaac's favorite because he was a hunter, "a man of the field," and Isaac loved the meat that he brought home. Jacob, however, was favored by Rebekah. He was "a quiet man, dwelling in tents" (vv. 27–28). When Isaac was old and ready to bestow his final blessing on his sons, Rebekah was mindful of God's prophecy, but either she worried it wouldn't happen or she imagined God needed her help. She conspired with Jacob to deceive Isaac, so that Jacob received the greater firstborn blessing Isaac intended to give to Esau (Genesis 27:1–29).

While this enriched Jacob, it enraged Esau so much that Rebekah sent her favorite son back to her homeland, far from Esau's reach. Jacob remained far from home with Rachel's brother, Laban, for many years.

Most of us can relate to Rebekah. When our desire for something in our lives is so powerful, we look for ways to make it a reality. Many of us offer a prayer but then imagine it's up to us to do the heavy lifting and make it happen.

We usually do have to take some action besides prayer. Hannah prayed with persistence, but of course she and Elkanah still had to act for the conception to occur. However, she invited God into her actions. If our own action, like Rebekah's deceit, is not in line with God's standards for behavior, we can be certain that is not the way He wants us to answer our own prayers. The old saying "God helps those who help themselves," often wrongly attributed to the Scriptures, actually flies in the face of the dependance God wants us to have on Him. Rebekah's actions created years of enmity between the brothers. It's a cautionary tale against taking matters into our own hands without investing in faith-filled prayer.

God desires a relationship of faith with His people. Persisting in prayer is an expression of that faith. Many Israelites took actions toward righteousness but didn't succeed. "Why? Because they did not pursue it by faith, but as if it were based on works" (Romans 9:32). Hannah made her requests known to God, then acted in faith. Rebekah acted on her own.

> God desires a relationship of faith with His people. Persisting in prayer is an expression of that faith.

Persistent prayer. Acting in line with God's commands. Patience and faith. These actions and attitudes don't make for exciting scenes on television, but they do make for fulfilling lives. Hannah demonstrated a godly path toward achieving blessed results that led straight through persistent prayer.

BIBLE

Read Hannah's story in 1 Samuel 1. Then read David's Psalm 6. What is the example both Hannah and David set with their prayers? What are some of the reasons God may ask us to be persistent in prayer?

Consider that Jesus even declared, "The Son can do nothing of his own accord, but only what he sees the Father doing. For whatever the Father does, that the Son does likewise" (John 5:19). And Paul warns us, "Do not be anxious about anything, but in everything by prayer and supplication with thanksgiving let your requests be made known to God" (Philippians 4:6). We can persist in prayer over one topic, praying until we see or sense an answer from God. We may also persist in prayer by continuing our practice of talking with God through prayer even when we haven't received the answers we desired.

Bible Extra

Second Chronicles 34 tells the story of King Josiah's repentance when the Book of the Law was found and read. He sent to the prophetess, Huldah, who told him all the prophecies of disaster resulting from the people's idolatry would come true. But "because your heart was tender and you humbled yourself before God when you heard his words against this place and its inhabitants, and you have humbled yourself before me and have torn your clothes and wept before me, I also have heard you, declares the LORD" (v. 27).

BATTLE

Does it sound like Hannah, David, Paul, or Josiah were people who prayed and then just sat around waiting for answers? What is the difference between working toward our God-given desires and manipulating circumstances using deception to achieve our own ends?

If we know God wants something done, as Rebekah did, what difference does it make how we "help it along"? This really is a battle for most of us, especially in times when the world dismisses thoughts and prayers as inconsequential. Praying is a power-filled action. God has much to say about the "how" of achieving the ends He desires.

This isn't one of those simple answers whereby we know exactly what to do in every situation. Instead, relying on prayer in all things and then listening for God's answer in His Word and through the Holy Spirit is the constant path we must walk. Stick with Hannah's choice and let the lasting influence of Rebekah's remind you to pray and not manipulate.

Bottom Line

Can we ever truly measure the impact of a woman committed to persistent, intensive prayer?

8

Herodias and Tabitha

The Impact of Service

Religion that is pure and undefiled before God the Father
is this: to visit orphans and widows in their affliction,
and to keep oneself unstained from the world.

James 1:27

I can't sew. Honestly, I've tried. There is a very patient group of quilters still rooting for me to persist, but sewing and handiwork are not at the top of my skill set (maybe not even at the bottom!). Still, I have great respect for people who serve with practical gifts—those who know how to grow food, raise animals, sew curtains, create quilts, and fix cars. Perhaps that is you.

Perhaps, like Tabitha (also known as Dorcas), you'll provide clothing for loved ones to wear, quilts for them to tuck under in the cold, or handcrafted tables at which they dine as part of your legacy. There is immense beauty in that. And strength. It's powerful to pass on items you've held in your hands, but especially those you created with those hands.

But if, like Tabitha, you employ your creative and practical gifts in service to the poor, ministering in concrete ways that touch hearts and provide for physical needs, then your influence could be eternal.

In this life, we all have a choice whether we'll serve others or serve our own selfish desires. Tabitha chose to serve others, and Peter raised her from the dead. How utterly unlike her was Herodias, wife of King Herod! In choosing to serve her own needs, Herodias orchestrated the death of John the Baptist.

Jesus loved His relative John, born six months prior to Him and called to prepare the way for the Lord. John was a wild prophet who unflinchingly preached repentance and called people to turn to God because His kingdom was at hand.

John didn't hesitate to call out sin. He did so publicly and regardless of the social status of the sinner. He called out the common man or woman listening to him as he baptized in the Jordan, but in vivid language he also called out Pharisees, religious leaders, and even the king.

John spoke against King Herod's relationship with Herodias because she was Herod's brother's wife. "And Herodias had a grudge against him and wanted to put him to death. But she could not, for Herod feared John, knowing that he was a righteous and holy man, and he kept him safe. When he heard him, he was greatly perplexed, and yet he heard him gladly" (Mark 6:19–20).

Here was a woman in an adulterous marriage, whose partner was reflecting on the words of God's prophet. She wanted that prophet silenced. Apparently, she liked her arrangement and the power it provided. We can imagine she appreciated the luxury and splendor of the palace and preferred it to repentance. In fact, these verses hint that she would have discouraged Herod from repenting.

It's easy to be shocked by what Herodias did next. We can distance ourselves from her actions because most of us couldn't imagine orchestrating anyone's death. And yet, in modern times, we don't have to resort to murder to silence God's prophets—those who clearly teach and proclaim His Word. We just don't listen. We change churches, switch channels, avoid certain gatherings, or decline to read certain books to avoid hearing what doesn't serve our selfish need to imagine we're fine without changing a thing.

No one would accuse Herodias of not demonstrating complete dedication to her own selfish ways. When Herod threw a banquet, Herodias's daughter danced for the guests. She was so pleasing that Herod promised to give her whatever she asked, "up to half of my kingdom" (Mark 6:23). She asked her mother what she should request. Here she was, on the verge of receiving riches, lands, gold, or jewels, but Herodias, her mother, wanted something above all else—to secure her own selfish desires. She told her daughter to ask for the head of John the Baptist.

> **In modern times, we don't have to resort to murder to silence God's prophets—those who clearly teach and proclaim His Word. We just don't listen.**

Beyond material wealth, some women want to get their own sinful ways and live without the nuisance of God's prophets telling them they're wrong. As for Herod, he was sorry he'd made his promise, but he clearly loved his pride more than doing what was honorable. God's great prophet lost his head because a self-centered man was unwilling to admit he'd made a foolish commitment and because a selfish woman chose to serve her own needs.

Herodias's legacy in the cause of serving herself is one of horror. She is a precursor of all who find God's truth so objectionable they will even murder to silence those who deliver it.

Various sources say the meaning of Herodias's name is "heroic" or "song of the hero." And to some in modern times, her commitment to self above all else is heroic. But it doesn't look heroic to destroy life and serve a dead man's head on a platter. It looks horrific.

It is no less horrific when we choose to live completely in the service of our own needs. Anytime we're tempted to demand someone's "head on a platter," whether for a poor business decision or a customer service error, we do well to remember Herodias and check our hearts.

Thank God for Tabitha. Tabitha, also known as Dorcas, means "gazelle" or "gracious." Tabitha lived in the service of others. In eight verses at the end of Acts 9, Luke gives us a glimpse of Tabitha's graceful influence.

First, he refers to her as a disciple living in Joppa, known today as Jaffa. It was a coastal city, also mentioned in the book of Jonah. Tabitha "was full of good works and acts of charity" (Acts 9:36). She was a believer in Jesus whose life demonstrated her faith. When she became ill and died, the disciples in Joppa sent for Peter, who was visiting a neighboring city.

When Peter arrived, the local widows stood beside Tabitha's body, weeping and showing him the tunics and other garments she had made for them. Peter sent them from the room and then, praying, raised Tabitha from the dead and presented her alive. This miracle became known throughout Joppa, and many believed in the Lord.

There is no evidence that the apostles resurrected every disciple who died. It's likely that Tabitha's service to the widows, who were probably poor, was well known in the bustling port city. Raising her from the dead was newsworthy. Her resurrection would have spread from business to tavern to town square. Thus was the gospel spread in Joppa.

In modern times, countless ministries to the vulnerable, poor, and outcast around the globe adopt Dorcas's name. One woman's practical, person-to-person ministry continues to help those in need and inspire many to spread the gospel with both word and deed.

I'm relieved to say (since I have no skills in that department) that Tabitha's choice wasn't exclusively about needlework. Her action was about serving the needs of others rather than serving her own needs. Even those of us who fumble in crafts or handiwork can choose to trust God with our own needs while we focus on meeting the needs of others. In this way we, like Peter, perpetuate Dorcas's ministry and ensure that the gospel is delivered with tangible demonstrations of love.

BIBLE

God clearly notices and values our service to others. Not only that, but He rewards this service. Conversely, God issues warnings about living for self.

Read what John has to say about Diotrephes in 3 John 1:9–11. Jesus warned that if we try to save our life, we will lose it, but if we lose our life for His sake, we will find it (Matthew 16:25). Herodias chose to orchestrate the death of another to preserve the comfortable life of sin she desired. Unless she repented later in life, that's all she will enjoy of life—that brief time, nothing more.

Bible Extra

Proverbs 19:17 says, "Whoever is generous to the poor lends to the LORD, and he will repay him for his deed." Hebrews 6:10 is like it: "God is not unjust; he will not forget your work and the love you have shown him as you have helped his people and continue to help them" (NIV). How do those verses encourage you?

BATTLE

No one will ever say it's easier to serve others rather than our own needs. All of us battle our inner desire to preserve our own lives every day. But God empowers us by His Holy Spirit to make better decisions, and He roots for us to live for Him.

When parents first see a child willing to share with another or willing to allow another child to go first, they recognize in their young one a mark of maturity and a glimmer that family values are being passed on. God searches our lives for those glimmers. Knowing this can be a motivational tool in our battle.

Jesus washed the feet of the apostles in the upper room on the night He was betrayed. Knowing that one of His own would betray Him and another would deny Him, Jesus still chose to serve each one. His power within us can strengthen us to serve others as well.

Bottom Line

Tabitha offered her life in service of others
and received it back from God. We too can
choose this self-giving path because of Jesus.

9

The Prostitute before Solomon, and Esther

The Impact of Selflessness

Where jealousy and selfish ambition exist, there will be disorder and every vile practice.

James 3:16

Discussing selflessness with women can be tricky.

Generations of women were raised to never consider their own needs and to only think of others, even to their personal detriment. Sometimes God's Word has been misapplied to shame women for asking others to respect their needs, skills, and dreams. Many have been silenced through social pressure, bullying, and sometimes abuse so that they fear advocating for themselves. As with other injustices, we rightly battle misapplications of Scripture that lead to minimizing or eradicating women's voices, contributions, and needs.

So when we discuss selflessness, we need to be sensitive that some will hear this message through the lens of historical or personal trauma. We must always frame the message of selflessness as being the responsibility of *every* believer. Believers of *both* genders, every ethnicity, tribe, and language, are charged by Christ, "If anyone would come after me, let him deny himself and take up his cross and follow me" (Matthew 16:24).

Jesus himself led the way in selfless living when He laid down His life for us. But He also rose from the dead and lives forever. He followed this charge of self-denial with this promise of life: "Whoever would save his life will lose it, but whoever loses his life for my sake will find it" (v. 25).

So wisdom is required when considering selflessness. It helps to contrast selflessness with selfishness. Reasonable people acknowledge it's not selfish to take care of oneself or to want to contribute to society using one's skills and talents. Selflessness, on the other hand, fully values our wants and needs but judiciously and freely sets them aside on behalf of another.

Selfish living leads to behaviors that shock us even when we believe we've seen and heard it all. But we can also find a purely selfless act shocking because of its rarity. Let's look at two women who made opposite but equally shocking choices.

First, a woman who chose selfishly. First Kings 3:16–28 records a story that illustrates the wisdom of Solomon. It involves a dispute between two women, pregnant prostitutes sharing a house—the only two in the home.

One woman gave birth first; the other delivered her child three days later. That night, the second woman rolled over on her newborn, and he died. She switched the infants so that the first woman awoke to a dead child. After the initial shock, the first mother realized it was not her son but belonged to the other woman.

The women brought their dispute to King Solomon. Both insisted the living child was hers. In those days long before DNA testing, the matter would seem impossible to settle . . . if it weren't for Solomon's wisdom.

With what we now know about postpartum grief, the actions of the dead child's mother might be, though not justifiable, at least explicable. Seeking to replace her lost son with a living one may have been the impulsive act of a bereaved woman. But she persisted in her deception. Arranging an audience with Solomon would have taken enough time for her to reconsider. Instead, she forged ahead, and then even before Solomon she stuck with her deceit.

Solomon ordered the disputed baby be cut in two, with one half given to each mother. The true mother petitioned for his life, requesting he be spared and given to the bereaved mother. That mother, however, agreed with Solomon's order to cut the child in two. Her selfish response testified to the truth she denied—she was not the mother of the living son. Solomon ordered the baby returned to the mother who would spare him.

It is natural to look to our own needs amid the challenges of life. Our traumas and trials can magnify that desire so that our attitudes become selfish and shockingly hurtful. From inside our own pain, we may even want others to suffer the way we suffer.

We never hear of this woman again in biblical history. But whenever her story is told, it serves as a warning to guard against harboring selfishness in our hearts, especially in the wake of loss or hardship, when we might be more susceptible to temptation.

The other prostitute demonstrated selflessness in her willingness to give up her child rather than see him killed, but another Old Testament woman was willing to lay down her own life for many: Esther.

Esther was born Hadassah, and by the time we meet her in Scripture, we know she's suffered loss because she's an orphan being raised by her cousin, Mordecai. They were Jews living, due to the dispersion, in what is modern-day Iran. A large Israelite community existed there in Susa, the citadel city, but they were foreigners nonetheless.

One day Vashti, queen of King Ahasuerus, failed to appear before him when ordered. Ahasuerus decreed he would choose a new queen from among the most beautiful virgins of the land.

And so Esther, because of her beauty, already a stranger in a strange land, was even taken from the only family she had, Mordecai.

He instructed Esther to keep her heritage a secret. So began twelve months of preparation for her one night with the king. In that time, despite all she had lost and suffered, Esther won the favor of those in charge. That speaks well of her character and carriage.

During her single night in the king's presence, Esther also won his favor and was crowned his new queen. But this was no Cinderella fairy tale. Esther had been forced into marriage to a man who followed idols. She was a minority living in a hostile land, compelled to deny her heritage and her family. And now she'd lost any other future she may have imagined for herself.

Yet the story indicates she did not let circumstances push her into bitterness or selfishness. And her selfless mindset would prove crucial to her people.

After a time, Esther's uncle, Mordecai, ran afoul of Haman, one of the king's officials, when he refused to obey a decree to pay homage to Haman. Haman, enraged, plotted to destroy not only Mordecai but all the Jews in the land. Haman tricked the king into issuing a decree to destroy them all in one day.

Mordecai sent word to Esther that she must appeal to the king on behalf of her people. Esther would be safe as no one knew her ethnicity, but her people would die. The decision to intervene was hers. Mordecai was certain God would deliver His people, but he suggested Esther might have been placed where she was "for such a time as this" (Esther 4:14).

Anyone who appeared before the king unsummoned risked death. Esther told Mordecai, "Go, gather all the Jews to be found in Susa, and hold a fast on my behalf, and do not eat or drink for three days, night or day. I and my young women will also fast as you do. Then I will go to the king, though it is against the law, and if I perish, I perish" (v. 16).

Esther, after three days of prayer and fasting, mustered the courage to go to her husband and plead for the lives of her people. Her selfless act delivered them from certain death—and Haman paid for his evil plot with his life.

Esther's selflessness led to life. She continues to inspire all to choose self*less*ness over self*ish*ness. Generations of Jews would not be here without the graceful influence of Esther's actions.

BIBLE

Read chapter 4 of Esther. Consider all that Esther had lost and suffered to that day. Consider all she'd gained being named queen and what she risked losing by interceding for her people. Then read Matthew 16:24–26. What is the long-lasting, eternal result of selflessly taking up your cross to follow Jesus?

Bible Extra

It's hard to imagine a woman so heartless she's willing to watch another woman's baby die. Thank God most of us don't live in such desperate times and situations that drive people to make such dreadful decisions. War can lead to this type of desperation. Second Kings 6:26–29 describes the Syrian siege of Samaria, which caused starvation so severe that two women resorted to cannibalism.

Terrible situations can set the stage for previously unthinkable choices. God can make the difference in our lives, so that, as with Esther, hardship and trial do not harden our hearts. All the more reason to pray for those facing persecution, terrorism, totalitarian regimes, and war.

BATTLE

Deciding to live selflessly and doing it is one of life's greatest battles.

In the garden of Gethsemane, Jesus asked the Father if there was another way than the cross. When there was none, Jesus selflessly obeyed God. His strength is available to us so we can make a better choice than the bereaved mother arguing before Solomon.

Selflessness can be counterfeited. Sometimes we realize we are serving others to be noticed, to earn love, or to control. Most of us won't be called to lay down our lives but we may need to set aside our agendas, preferences, or comforts to serve others. True selflessness happens when we act for another person's best interests knowing we have nothing to gain.

God's training comes through His Word and through encountering both encouragement and trials. We can cooperate and allow Him to fill our hearts with what filled His when He laid down His life for us. His presence in our hearts is our hope, in this battle of selflessness, that as we allow Him greater influence on our spirits, we will become like Him. Then as we lose our lives, we will find them.

Bottom Line

Esther's selflessness led to life for
many and continues to inspire all to
selflessness over selfishness.

Rachel and Achsah

The Impact of Asking

*She said to him, "Give me a blessing. Since you have given
me the land of the Negeb, give me also springs of water."
And he gave her the upper springs and the lower springs.*

Joshua 15:19

When my father was dying and making final decisions
about possessions, I listened for a long time before
realizing one item was especially important to me. I'd
spent years being quiet around my parents about my needs, but
finally one day I asked.

My father looked surprised.

"I'm sorry," I said, "you don't have to leave it to me."

He just shook his head. "It's not that. Of course you can have
it. I just don't remember you ever asking for much. Things aren't
often important to you. It's yours."

Little did I know that in the family turmoil following his
death, that item would bring me great comfort. More than my
possessing it, though, was the fact that all I had to do was ask,
and my father was happy to give. That was strong solace.

Jesus's brother James wrote about asking. He was the straight-
talking leader of the church in Jerusalem. The book of James is

frank and direct: "You do not have, because you do not ask" (James 4:2).

God wants us to ask, to make requests, to petition Him for our needs. In the prayer Jesus taught His disciples, He instructed us to ask for daily bread, for forgiveness, and for deliverance. Of course, God knows what we need, but He instructs us to ask.

Two Old Testament women, Rachel and Achsah, wanted something from their fathers. One stole. One asked.

If Jacob's wife Rachel were on Facebook, every relationship status would be captioned, "It's complicated." Complicated marriage, complicated sister relationship, and complicated father-daughter interactions. Worse, Rachel was surrounded by men who were in the habit of taking, not asking. These were the leadership examples she had in her life, just to set her decisions in context.

Jacob, her husband, and Laban, her father, were cut from the same cloth, so to speak. Jacob, his mother's favorite son, hoodwinked his father for his blessing and had to flee his brother Esau's wrath. It seems only fitting that such a manipulator would become entangled with his uncle Laban, himself a practiced wheeler-dealer.

Jacob fell immediately in love with Rachel, Laban's beautiful daughter, and brokered a deal to work seven years for her hand in marriage. At the wedding, however, Laban disguised his older daughter, Leah, as the bride.

In the morning, when the trickery was discovered, Laban agreed Jacob could have both daughters, but Jacob would have to work another seven years for Rachel. Sadly, Leah was unloved, but God blessed her with children. Rachel was adored but struggled with infertility.

Eventually she gave birth to Joseph but then died giving birth to Jacob's youngest son, Benjamin. Leah's and Rachel's twelve sons (by birth and by claim through their handmaids, Zilpah and Bilhah) would become the twelve tribes of Israel.

Eventually, Jacob's family became a threat to Laban's sons, so with God's blessing, Jacob planned to leave Laban and return home with his wives, children, servants, and flocks. Jacob explained to the sisters that their father had not dealt with him with integrity, so they would pack and flee while Laban was away shearing sheep.

Rachel and Leah replied, "Is there any portion or inheritance left to us in our father's house? Are we not regarded by him as foreigners? For he has sold us, and he has indeed devoured our money. All the wealth that God has taken away from our father belongs to us and to our children. Now then, whatever God has said to you, do" (Genesis 31:14–16).

The family packed everything up on camels and gathered all the livestock. In addition, "Rachel stole her father's household gods" (v. 19).

We can only speculate as to why she desired these items. Perhaps she was worried about relying on Jacob's God alone. Perhaps she hoped they would secure her, as their holder, legal claim to Laban's wealth when he died. Some have wondered if she wanted to push Laban into trusting Jacob's God. Surrounded as she was by dealmakers and manipulators, I would wager that was not the case. Jacob believed in God, but his actions didn't always testify to faith that God would provide.

The theft nearly cost Rachel her life. When Laban came after them, demanding the return of the idols, Jacob declared that whoever possessed them would be killed. Rachel hid them under her saddle and claimed she couldn't rise because "the way of women" was upon her. So, she retained possession of them. One wrong leads to another and another.

Rachel's decision to steal rather than to ask is representative of all who rely on their own methods to obtain what they need rather than ask. Of course, Rachel's father was himself unreliable and clearly selfish; when Jacob had asked him for Rachel in marriage, Laban instead delivered Leah. So we can understand why his daughter had no faith in asking him for anything. Their relationship exemplifies the brokenness of a world without God.

A world of untrustworthy fathers and of daughters who take what they want rather than ask for it.

Achsah's story is also about a father, a husband, and a daughter with a need, but it is characterized by faith. Caleb, Achsah's father, was one of the twelve spies Moses sent into the promised land. Of the twelve, only he and Joshua had faith that God would help them overcome the giants in the land.

As the Israelites battled their way into the territory God promised them, it's possible Caleb sought someone of similar faith for his daughter. He promised Achsah to whoever captured the territory they currently faced. His nephew Othniel proved worthy, and Caleb gave the couple land in the Negeb, a desert territory.

Achsah, confident in her father's love, assessed their need and asked her father to also give her springs of water. Caleb granted her request and gave her more than she needed.

Here we have a beautiful image of relationships in proper order: a father of faith marrying his daughter to a man of faith, and a daughter confident she can request what she needs.

> **God rejects our sin, but He doesn't reject our humanity.**

This is a foreshadowing of Christ, who would one day meet with a Samaritan woman at Jacob's well. There He would tell her that if she asked, He would give her "living water." That water "will become in him a spring of water welling up to eternal life" for whoever drinks it (John 4:14). We have a Father of whom we can ask whatever we need.

God rejects our sin, but He doesn't reject our humanity. It is human to want. Human to have needs. Human to ask—for help, for resources, for understanding, for what we want.

Achsah serves to remind us that children of God have faith to ask, and so to receive. Our good Father is worthy of our trust.

Rachel's sons, Joseph and Benjamin, were comforts to their

father, and God used Joseph to deliver his family from famine. They are part of Rachel's legacy. Rachel, however, died in sorrow on the way to Bethlehem giving birth to Benjamin. She represents inconsolable sorrow in another time recorded in the New Testament. After Jesus was born, Herod ordered the death of all male children under two. So it was that "'a voice was heard in Ramah, weeping and loud lamentation, Rachel weeping for her children; she refused to be comforted, because they are no more'" (Matthew 2:18). Rachel, who relied on her manipulations, epitomized all who mourned when King Herod, through his own machinations, tried to destroy the King of the universe.

One lesson we learn from Achsah and Rachel is the power of asking for what we need. But more than that, we can see the importance of having faith in the One we ask.

BIBLE

Second Kings 4 describes two women with the confidence to ask. One widow sought Elisha's help when her dead husband's creditors demanded to take her children into slavery. Elisha instructed her to gather all her empty vessels and ask her neighbors for theirs as well. Then she was to go into her home and begin pouring the little oil she had into those containers. She obeyed, and the oil didn't run out until all the containers were full. She sold the oil, paid her debts, and saved her children (vv. 1–7).

The second widow, a Shunammite woman, showed hospitality to Elisha, and God blessed her with a son in return. When the son was older, he suddenly died. The woman went to Elisha asking for help, and he delivered the boy from death (vv. 8–37). When have you asked for what you've needed and received a good response? The result of asking in faith for what we need can influence generations that follow.

Bible Extra

Genesis 19:30–38 tells the story of Lot and his daughters following the destruction of Sodom and Gomorrah. Lot's wife turned to salt for looking back after they were warned not to look back. Lot "went up out of Zoar and lived in the hills with his two daughters, for he was afraid to live in Zoar. So he lived in a cave with his two daughters." He was a father living in fear.

Possibly because their father fearfully chose to hide in a cave rather than go into another city, his daughters didn't know any better than to think all other men had been destroyed. Rather than ask how they would have their own children (who knows how he was acting in the wake of all that destruction), they chose to get Lot drunk and have sexual relations with him, each in turn. The resulting nations, the Ammonites and Moabites, would prove to be challenging neighbors for the Israelites for many years.

BATTLE

The battle in the decision to ask is multilayered. First, we must have faith that God is a loving Father and not a father of manipulations like Laban. It's easier to take our cues from those around us, like Rachel, and align our thinking with theirs, but it's not wiser. Meditate on God's goodness demonstrated throughout His Word.

Second, we must ask in faith for what we need, not for selfish gain. Working with the Holy Spirit to know what to pray helps sort out our needs from our self-centered wants. Listen to the Holy Spirit and pray accordingly.

Bottom Line

God rejects our sin, not our humanity.
Ask Him for what you need.

Hagar and Shiphrah and Puah

The Impact of Faith

Without faith it is impossible to please him, for whoever would draw near to God must believe that he exists and that he rewards those who seek him.

Hebrews 11:6

Invisibility can happen at any stage of life. I experienced it when my daughter became a young adult. She is a beauty, and while I'm no slouch, I felt myself fade in her presence.

One day, I purchased us each a coffee as my daughter stood beside me. I did the ordering, the receiving, and the paying. During the entire transaction, however, the young man only had eyes for Hannah. He and I never even made eye contact. Once at a restaurant, our waiter was so enamored of her, she and I had to switch water glasses so mine would be filled!

This invisibility made me giggle and roll my eyes. It wasn't painful. But I certainly have experienced pain from feeling invisible. Several times helping my older parents, we encountered friends of my mother who greeted us with surprise. "I didn't know you had a daughter. You've only ever spoken about your son." Ouch.

When we feel invisible to others, it's easy to imagine we're also invisible to God. It requires faith to trust that God sees us, especially when our circumstances are oppressive and it seems our prayers are unheard. Choosing to walk in the faith that we are seen by God even when life is at its worst is so hard. But the rewards may extend beyond ourselves even to generations to come.

Hagar lived a life over which she had little control. An Egyptian woman, she was Sarai's maidservant, likely acquired during Sarai and Abram's time in Egypt. She lived with them as they followed their God to a land He had promised them. Hagar was a woman far from home serving a people who weren't her people.

As we've said, if the Bible were fiction, it would be full of heroes and heroines, good guys and bad. It's not fiction, though, so apart from the truly evil, it isn't easy (or wise) to categorize people into purely good or bad. Mostly, they were just imperfect, sinful people navigating life within the context of the times, cultures, and situations they were given. God is the hero of every story, and He was that for Hagar.

Despite God's promise to Abram that his offspring would outnumber the stars, Sarai struggled with infertility, so she took the situation in hand. In the custom of the times, Sarai sent Hagar to Abram in the hopes that she would conceive a child on Sarai's behalf.

When Hagar did conceive, she "looked with contempt" (Genesis 16:4) on Sarai. That's only a short phrase, but it's a powerful expression of the change in their relationship. Other translations say Hagar "lost respect for" or "despised" Sarai. The New American Standard Bible says Sarai became "insignificant in her sight."

It doesn't require much imagination to consider Sarai's pain of longing to have a child with Abram, only to have Hagar conceive. Sarai's decision (and Abram's assent) disrupted the relational power structure of the household, creating a painful situation for

Sarai, which she then turned back on Hagar. Sarai had authored a dynamic that put her at risk of invisibility in her own household. A self-inflicted wound is still a wound; however, despite her pain, she could have addressed the matter without becoming harsh.

Sarai complained to Abram, who dismissed Sarai to handle Hagar as she wished. Sarai "dealt harshly" with Hagar. (Some translations say Sarai was "cruel to," "mistreated," "oppressed," or "afflicted" her.) It was so unbearable, Hagar ran away.

When working with families in crisis, I've heard people accuse other family members of being wrong and try to make the case that they are right. Then the other person arrives and does the same. I have frequently held up my hand to silence the accusations. "It's quite possible that everyone here is wrong," I'd say. That was the situation with Sarai, Abram, and Hagar.

Why wouldn't Hagar run? She'd served this family and knew Abram was favored by his God. Sarai was also known to Abram's God. But Hagar, a servant, had no faith that she was known to this invisible God of theirs, and she was far from the gods of Egypt.

She probably knew she shouldn't have looked on Sarai with contempt, having witnessed the pain barrenness brought her. But Sarai also shouldn't have treated Hagar harshly. Abram could have led in wiser ways. Hagar was surrounded by wrong, and she was powerless, so she ran. She understandably didn't have faith that she was personally visible to Abram's God.

God, however, surprised Hagar by appearing to her in the wilderness. God spoke with Hagar just as He had with Abram and Sarai.

He sent Hagar back to face her situation but promised that her son had a future and that *her* offspring, too, would be multiplied, a promise like the one God had made Abram. He told Hagar, "I will surely multiply your offspring so that they cannot be numbered for multitude" (Genesis 16:10).

"Behold, you are pregnant and shall bear a son," God continued.

"You shall call his name Ishmael, because the LORD has listened to your affliction" (v. 11). Ishmael would indeed become the father of twelve sons (25:12–18), who were known as the Ishmaelites.

Hagar called God *El Roi*, "the God who sees me." She was not invisible; she was seen. "Truly here I have seen him who looks after me" (v. 13).

When Hagar felt invisible, she made the nearly disastrous decision to run away to the wilderness. Once God assured her that she was seen, she placed her faith in Him. Then she had the courage to choose life for her son, Ishmael. Faith that we are seen by the Living God leads to thinking and actions that bring all kinds of life, not only for us but also often for others.

Centuries after Hagar's wilderness encounter with God, the nation of Israel had become enslaved to the pharaoh of Egypt. The tables had turned, and now the women of Israel were the ones in bondage. They were the servants to the Egyptians. Rather than infertility, the problem for the Israelites now was, they were multiplying in such numbers that Pharaoh grew fearful of an uprising.

To slow the birth rate of the Hebrew children, Pharaoh treated them harshly. "But the more they were oppressed, the more they multiplied and the more they spread abroad. And the Egyptians were in dread of the people of Israel. So they ruthlessly made the people of Israel work as slaves and made their lives bitter with hard service, in mortar and brick, and in all kinds of work in the field. In all their work they ruthlessly made them work as slaves" (Exodus 1:12–14).

These measures failed in limiting the Hebrew population, so Pharaoh summoned the Hebrew midwives, Shiphrah and Puah. He directed them to kill the newborn sons when the Jewish women gave birth.

In those days, childbirth was women's work and women's business—not a place for kings. Even though their work was done in private, Shiphrah and Puah knew they were not invisible to the Living God. This faith informed their choice to defy the king, who could easily take their lives. "The midwives feared God and did not do as the king of Egypt commanded them, but let the male children live" (v. 17).

When the king challenged them after learning that the Hebrew sons were surviving, the midwives covered to save their lives, knowing they answered to a higher King. Verses 20 and 21 tell something of the effects of their faith in action: "So God dealt well with the midwives. And the people multiplied and grew very strong. And because the midwives feared God, he gave them families."

Each of the three women in this chapter, living in bondage, had a choice: either act in fear that she was invisible to God, or act in faith that she was seen and lived under His care. When Hagar, Shiphrah, and Puah acted on faith, the outcome was life—lives, in fact, that spawned entire generations. Along with their faith also came reward.

BIBLE

The author of Hebrews writes, "Without faith it is impossible to please him, for whoever would draw near to God must believe that he exists and that he rewards those who seek him" (Hebrews 11:6). You believe God exists, but do you also believe that He rewards those who seek Him? What does this mean to you?

Read Exodus 2:1–10. Moses's mother, Jochabed, exercised faith by putting the infant Moses in the river. Pharaoh's daughter was one reward for this faith when she saw the child, drew him out, and raised him to adulthood.

Bible Extra

I've often wondered about "the other Mary" mentioned in Matthew 27:61 and 28:1. Jesus loved her and knew her, but Matthew simply refers to her as "the other Mary." That may imply insignificance, but "the other Mary" heard the announcement from the angel at the empty tomb. What a privilege! She was not invisible or insignificant to God.

What faith do you have that God sees you? Read Psalm 33:18; 1 Peter 3:12; and 1 Samuel 16:7. Meditate on these passages this week and ask God to increase your faith that He sees you. How could this affect your thoughts, feelings, and actions? How might this truth that God sees you inspire faith?

BATTLE

One of our enemy's most frequently used tactics is to convince us our lives don't matter. We begin to imagine that God only watches "spiritual giants" or Christian leaders. We start to believe our small lives don't add up to much and don't merit His attention.

The Bible tells a different story, and God himself states the truth that we are seen. The faith that our actions do matter, that God does see us, and that He does reward those who seek Him can empower us to make choices that influence entire nations.

Bottom Line

Faith that we are seen by the Living God leads to thinking and actions that bring all kinds of life, not only for us but also often for others.

12

Potiphar's Wife and Rahab

The Impact of Courage

Have I not commanded you? Be strong and courageous.
Do not be frightened, and do not be dismayed, for
the LORD your God is with you wherever you go.

Joshua 1:9

S tories of great courage are retold throughout generations, often because those generations may not have existed if it weren't for that courage. Courage does indeed inspire and affect generations.

Oskar Schindler is a controversial figure, but in 2019, children of people who survived the Holocaust because of his brave actions gathered to honor him. According to *The Times of Israel*, one woman in attendance, Lea Guterman, "said her parents, saved by Schindler, 'raised five children. Those five children reared 36 grandchildren and over 120 or 150 great-grandchildren—after 120 we stopped counting.'"[4] Guterman's parents were only two of the 1,200 Jews alive because of Schindler's courageous actions and that of his clerk, Itzak Stern.

Corrie ten Boom, like Schindler, shines for her courage, along with her sister, Betsie, their father, Casper, and other family members who became part of the Dutch underground during World War II. Motivated by their faith, they hid Jews in their home to help them escape capture by the Nazis. The family was eventually discovered, arrested, and held at Scheveningen prison, where Casper died.

Corrie and Betsie were subsequently sent to Ravensbruck concentration camp. Betsie lost her life in the camp but, due to a clerical error, Corrie survived. She recorded their story in her book *The Hiding Place* and devoted years of her life to writing and speaking around the world about the love and forgiveness of Jesus Christ.

Two Bible women, Potiphar's wife and Rahab, made radically different decisions. The lying cowardice of the one sent a man to jail. The other's protective bravery, inspired by faith in the God of the Israelites, guarded Joshua's spies, securing their escape from capture and, as a reward, saving her family's lives.

Potiphar's wife has held fascination beyond the Hebrew Scriptures. The biblical account in Genesis 39 is repeated in the histories of Josephus and mentioned also in other ancient literature. There are many lessons to learn from this woman's choices, but we're focusing on her lack of courage.

Joseph had been the victim of treachery by his jealous older brothers, having been sold as a slave to passing Ishmaelites. Potiphar, captain of the guard for Egypt's Pharaoh, bought Joseph. God was with the young man and, because of that, Potiphar prospered. So did his entire household, so that Joseph was trusted and given much responsibility.

The Bible tells us that Joseph was handsome. He caught the eye of Potiphar's wife. Who knows her situation? Was she unloved? Was she bored? It really doesn't matter. One thing we know for certain is that she was married, but day after day she asked Joseph to lie with her.

To his credit, Joseph refused, citing the trust Potiphar had in him and the sinfulness of adultery. She persisted. The text implies determination, not an impulse or a momentary weakness—highlighting that Joseph persistently resisted her advances. He didn't weaken.

Finally, on a day when no other men were in the house, she grabbed at his clothing. This time he ran away, leaving her holding his robe. Perhaps she realized that when he ran outside without it, the men working there might notice and make assumptions.

So, preemptively, she lied.

Potiphar's wife chose the cowardice of false testimony. The spinelessness of refusing to take responsibility for her own behavior. Her blame shifting was much like Adam's when he and Eve were discovered in their sin. Potiphar's wife ran to the workers and placed responsibility not only on Joseph but also on the man who brought Joseph into their lives, her own husband. She accused Joseph of doing what she had attempted to do and laid the blame on everyone except herself.

Placed in an untenable position by her public accusations, Potiphar threw Joseph into prison. Because of this woman's actions, Joseph spent two years there. Revictimized. Once again, he suffered consequences for the sinful choices of others, just as he had when his brothers acted against him. Still, he endured these trials with unwavering faith in God. For Joseph, the result of Potiphar's wife's cowardice was at least those two years in prison.

We can speculate about other motives besides self-preservation. Lust. Entitlement. Pride. Selfishness. Regardless, what she did was cowardly. It surprises many to find the Bible lists cowards beside murderers and idolators: "As for the cowardly, the faithless, the detestable, as for murderers, the sexually immoral, sorcerers, idolaters, and all liars, their portion will be in the lake that burns with fire and sulfur, which is the second death" (Revelation 21:8). The story of Joseph and Potiphar's wife illustrates how lacking the courage to take responsibility for our behavior can negatively impact other people's lives in terrible ways.

By God's providence, Joseph found freedom and rose to a position of power to save his family and his people from famine. He suffered, but God used every circumstance to work out His sovereign plan.

Rahab's story beautifully illustrates the graceful influence of courage. Her story is told in the book of Joshua and took place when the Israelites were entering the promised land. Word of God's miraculous deliverance of His people from Egypt had preceded them (Joshua 2:10–11). The leaders of Jericho prepared to battle Israel, but the Israelites knew their God was capable of mighty works on their behalf.

Rahab was a prostitute in Jericho. She had heard of the God of the Israelites and had come to acknowledge Him as "God in the heavens above and on the earth beneath" (Joshua 2:11). So when two of Joshua's spies sent in ahead of the armies came to her, Rahab hid them. She directed their pursuers sent by the king of Jericho away from their hiding place.

Once the spies were in the clear, Rahab brokered a deal for her family's safety. Before helping them escape the city, the spies agreed to protect Rahab and her family on the day Israel attacked Jericho. So that Israel would recognize Rahab's house, which was built into the city wall, the spies told her to tie a scarlet cord to her window. In this way they could keep their promise.

God brought down the walls of Jericho and gave Israel the victory over that city. Before setting it on fire, Joshua ordered the spies to rescue Rahab and all her loved ones. "Rahab the prostitute and her father's household and all who belonged to her, Joshua saved alive. And she has lived in Israel to this day, because she hid the messengers whom Joshua sent to spy out Jericho" (Joshua 6:25). In sheltering the spies from harm, Rahab had chosen courage inspired by faith in a God she couldn't see. Her backbone saved her family.

Rahab not only risked her life to protect God's men, but she also courageously followed a new God, trusting Him to deliver her family. She was brave enough to begin again with a people who weren't her people, following God into a new culture, new relationships, and an entirely new life.

The influence of Rahab's bravery extends into the New Testament. Tucked into the first genealogy in Matthew 1 are these words in verses 5–6: "Salmon the father of Boaz by Rahab, and Boaz the father of Obed by Ruth, and Obed the father of Jesse, and Jesse the father of David the king." Rahab was given a family of her own, becoming the grandmother of kings, and was ultimately included in the line of the Messiah.

Everyday acts of courage, like telling the truth even when it's hard, starting a new job or ministry, making friends with people different from us, or setting healthy boundaries can prepare us for times that call for even greater bravery, such as facing persecution.

BIBLE

After Stephen was martyred, the Bible says, "There arose on that day a great persecution against the church in Jerusalem, and they were all scattered throughout the regions of Judea and Samaria, except the apostles. Devout men buried Stephen and made great lamentation over him. But Saul was ravaging the church, and entering house after house, he dragged off men and women and committed them to prison" (Acts 8:1–3).

> It takes courage to be willing for people to think less of us.

Times of persecution, when publicly acknowledging Jesus can result in loss of work, arrest, and even death, require courage. But so do lesser risks. It takes courage to share the gospel with a friend, state an unpopular truth, or simply be willing for people to think less of us.

Read Mark 15:42–43. Why did Joseph of Arimathea need courage to approach Pilate on Jesus's behalf, and what do these verses say motivated him? Read also Hebrews 11:13–16. What do these verses say about the faith and courage required to move away from what is familiar and move toward the coming kingdom? When might it require courage just to risk people's disapproval, loss of friends, or a change in social status?

Bible Extra

Jesus said, "I tell you, my friends, do not fear those who kill the body, and after that have nothing more that they can do. But I will warn you whom to fear: fear him who, after he has killed, has authority to cast into hell. Yes, I tell you, fear him!" (Luke 12:4–5). This fear of God is about revering Him or respecting Him above all else. How have you seen a "fear of God" inspire courage in your life?

BATTLE

There are real things to fear in this life. Some fears are easier to manage, like risking a family member's disapproval or attempting a new ministry. Costlier fears, like risking our lives, require more serious consideration. Those Christians who made brave choices in war likely also practiced lesser braveries before they even knew war was coming. As in all things, we can rely on the Holy Spirit to supply what we need in the moment we need it. Our belief in the coming kingdom of Jesus Christ, fueled by love for God, can rightly prioritize our fears so that our fear of God takes prominence and motivates courage.

There's nothing easy about choosing courage over cowardice, but there is a coming reward.

Bottom Line

The cost of cowardice is far-reaching, but the reward of courage ripples through generations.

Michal and Anna

The Impact of Worship

God is spirit, and those who worship him
must worship in spirit and truth.

John 4:24

There are so many demands on our time. It's easy to let worship slip lower on our priority list.

It's true we aren't saved by attending a weekly church service. Jesus saves, not church attendance. But when we come to Christ, we become part of a body of believers, and God's Word makes clear we are to gather regularly (Hebrews 10:24–25). We need one another. We belong with one another.

Worship occurs in a church service, but that's not the exclusive opportunity for worship. We can worship corporately, individually, or wherever "two or three are gathered" in Jesus's name (Matthew 18:20). We worship with music, prayer, reading and hearing God's Word, preaching, and giving. Paul tells us to "present your bodies as a living sacrifice, holy and acceptable to God, which is your spiritual worship" (Romans 12:1). Worship clearly isn't contained within the walls of our sanctuaries.

Worship is truly an attitude of the heart, a position we take in the universe, an internal response to God that we outwardly express in a variety of ways. Worship may involve silence or singing, kneeling or dancing, learning and listening to God's Word, and living according to what we've learned. Essentially, worship is what occurs when we rightly respond to God, either alone or with others.

Christians can get frustrated with one another over varying forms of worship. We have conflicts over what worship entails, how often worship should occur and where, and how to reflect preferences in corporate worship. In all the debate, we can become discouraged or confused enough to neglect worship. That's a mistake. There is power and strength that leads to resilience when we regularly focus our attention on God and allow our bodies, minds, and spirits to respond with reverence and awe.

> **Worship is truly an attitude of the heart, a position we take in the universe, an internal response to God that we outwardly express in a variety of ways.**

Michal's reaction to her husband King David's effusive worship had a lasting outcome in her life. The prophetess Anna's decades-long devotion to worship also reaped powerful results for her, culminating in an encounter with the Messiah.

King Saul's younger daughter, Michal, loved David. This was convenient for her father, who was jealous of David's heroic battle conquests. He hoped Michal would become a snare for David. Being married to the daughter of the king would increase his value as a target for their enemies.

In a way, it proved true, but not because it increased the Philistines' desire to kill David. Instead, when Saul saw that David was loved by God *and* by his daughter, it made him even more determined to eliminate him as a rival. This made for an understandably complex relationship between the three.

Throughout most of their story, Michal was a loyal and supportive wife to David—until the return of the ark of the covenant. In 2 Samuel 6, the ark remained in the house of Obed-edom the Gittite. The ark had appeared so holy it was dangerous to have near. But when David saw how God blessed Obed-edom's household, he was willing to bring it to the city of David.

The day the ark was carried through the streets was filled with celebration. David danced before God while all the people proceeded with great shouting and the sound of the horn (2 Samuel 6:14–15). Michal apparently didn't appreciate David's unselfconscious display. "As the ark of the LORD came into the city of David, Michal the daughter of Saul looked out of the window and saw King David leaping and dancing before the LORD, and she despised him in her heart" (v. 16).

The ark was brought to its place. There David offered burnt offerings and peace offerings. He blessed the people in the Lord's name, and everyone enjoyed some bread, meat, and raisin cake before retiring. But when David returned home, Michal's scorn awaited him. "How the king of Israel honored himself today, uncovering himself today before the eyes of his servants' female servants, as one of the vulgar fellows shamelessly uncovers himself!" (v. 20). The Bible does note that David was only wearing a "linen ephod" (v. 14), meaning he'd set aside his royal robes to worship exuberantly.

Sadly, similar scenes are repeated in many homes today. One member of a family returns home, having delighted in God through worship, only to be immediately greeted by someone ready to tear that worship down.

Even though Michal loved David, it's possible she also valued her royal status and her respected station in life above devotion to God. David's "vulgar" display before everyone had possibly embarrassed her or created discomfort. Maybe a hint of jealousy brewed in her heart. Perhaps the enemy of her soul tempted Michal to scorn in the hope it would sober David and restrain his worship in the future.

David escaped that snare. He responded, "It was before the LORD, who chose me above your father and above all his house, to appoint me as prince over Israel, the people of the LORD—and I will celebrate before the LORD. I will make myself yet more contemptible than this, and I will be abased in your eyes. But by the female servants of whom you have spoken, by them I shall be held in honor" (vv. 21–22).

David recognized the fault here resided in Michal's heart alone. She had chosen not to join in worship and found herself left out. He rejected the shame her words were intended to incite. It seems that the final word on their exchange is that Michal had no child until her death (v. 23). Such was the intensely personal, lasting influence of Michal's despising her husband's public worship. We don't hear of her again in the biblical account.

Anna's story is shorter and quieter but profound. "There was a prophetess, Anna, the daughter of Phanuel, of the tribe of Asher. She was advanced in years, having lived with her husband seven years from when she was a virgin, and then as a widow until she was eighty-four. She did not depart from the temple, worshiping with fasting and prayer night and day" (Luke 2:36–37).

If Anna married at fourteen or fifteen, as was tradition, it's conceivable that she spent over sixty years worshiping daily in the temple. Her worship often consisted of fasting and praying.

Perhaps people noticed her as a young widow, but at some time in all those decades, she probably began to blend into the temple fixtures. Maybe they referred to her as "the worshiping widow" or "the woman who prays daily at the temple." All we know is that she devoted herself to the worship of the Lord.

Then in verse 37, Luke tells us of Anna's reward: she was there when Jesus's parents presented Him at the temple as an infant.

"And coming up at that very hour she began to give thanks to God and to speak of him to all who were waiting for the redemption of Jerusalem."

Anna, a widowed, worshiping prophetess, was blessed to meet the Savior of the world and to tell of Him to all who would listen. She who devoted her life to worship was privileged to witness the long-awaited infant Messiah.

Who knows the full effect of her words? Who knows how many lives began their walk toward the Messiah because of her report? And who knows what influence she had on the people who had witnessed her daily devotion for decades?

What is your practice of worship? What do those around you say about your worship habits? Anna's graceful influence is to illustrate that God receives and rewards our worship, whether it involves public exuberance or daily fasting and prayer. Though widowed at a time and place where widowhood would normally have left Anna destitute, her life appears to have been anything but that.

Worship of the Living God has the power to transform lives. It humbles the high and elevates the lowly to respond rightly to the God of the universe, the creator of all things. It enriches us. Our habit of worship can be the signpost that guides the way for others to His throne.

BIBLE

Read Psalm 29, written by David. What does it mean to "worship the LORD in the splendor of holiness" (v. 2)? What are the places, practices, and supports that lead your heart to worship? Is it music, art, or architecture? Is it nature? Is it silence? Is it being with God's people? Or is it God's Word alone? Where are the opportunities in your week to worship either alone or corporately? How can you protect that space to ensure worship is a regular practice?

Bible Extra

Read Hebrews 10:23–25. What is the impact of your worship on the others in your household, faith community, or neighborhood? How can that fortify you to continue in worship when tempted to withdraw? Pray for opportunities to invite others to worship with you. When you read about the multitude worshiping before the throne of God in Revelation 7:9–12, what does it do for your heart to picture women and men from every nation, tribe, people, and language praising God together there?

BATTLE

There's no mention of Michal objecting to routine worship that followed their traditional practice. Her battle occurred when she witnessed worship she deemed inappropriate. David worshiped from his heart, but that's clearly not what mattered to Michal.

Her battle was that of every one of us who witnesses a loving display of worship. Do we join with it, even if we are uncomfortable with the style, humbly desiring the same exuberance for God? Or do we find ways to pick at the person or people, rejecting the way they display their response to God?

Anna clearly had some trials early in her life, but she turned to God in worship and discovered a richness there. Will we choose worship in every circumstance? Will we worship focused solely on God, forgetting what others may see?

Bottom Line

Our habit of worship can be the signpost that
guides the way for others to His throne.

Noah's Wife and Lot's Wife

The Impact of Looking Forward

*One thing I do: forgetting what lies behind and straining
forward to what lies ahead, I press on toward the goal
for the prize of the upward call of God in Christ Jesus.*

Philippians 3:13–14

I confess that for most of my life, I judged Lot's wife harshly. I mean, who turns to look back at the destruction of Sodom and Gomorrah? Why not keep focused on what's ahead?

Through the years, however, God has delivered me from some unhealthy, difficult situations, and I had to admit to a similar struggle. The challenge of moving forward into transition, change, and all that is unfamiliar, with a focus only on Jesus and what lies ahead . . . whew! Those experiences provided a new perspective. Not clinging to what is behind us can be hard.

Even when situations and people behind us aren't good for us, something inside resists the forward move. Memory softens sharp edges as the reality of beginning again stares us straight in the eyes.

Circumstances can erode our confidence that we are strong enough to make a change. We can lose ourselves in trying conditions and become so numb we forget we are capable of moving in new directions.

I've asked forgiveness for judging Lot's wife. Okay, and for similarly judging the children of Israel. I've asked forgiveness for looking down on the Israelites in the wilderness as they bemoaned their deliverance from Egypt. They were wrong, but I can fall prey to that temptation just as they did.

Lot's wife died without entering her deliverance, and the generation that complained in the wilderness died shy of the promised land. They were all looking back. They were trying to recapture lives that, by God's mercy, they'd left behind.

There are certainly times when God commanded the Israelites to look back or to remember (Psalm 78). The reason for that remembrance, though, was not to be wistful and live in the past, but to recall God's faithfulness to fuel the faith needed to press on. Solomon cautions us, "Say not, 'Why were the former days better than these?' For it is not from wisdom that you ask this" (Ecclesiastes 7:10). Paul also set a forward-looking example. "One thing I do: forgetting what lies behind and straining forward to what lies ahead, I press on toward the goal for the prize of the upward call of God in Christ Jesus" (Philippians 3:13–14).

Jesus referenced Lot's wife directly: "Remember Lot's wife. Whoever seeks to preserve his life will lose it, but whoever loses his life will keep it" (Luke 17:32–33). He knew we could all be tempted as she was. Even if we recognized the culture around us had become completely godless and our neighbors were a constant danger, we might have grown so attached to our homes, comforts, and knowing where to buy the best cut of lamb that we struggled not to look back when God called us out. Or, like the wandering Israelites, one too many manna casseroles or another night cleaning sand from our hair and we too would be reminiscing about the good times living under Pharaoh.

We all need Jesus. He is our source of strength to choose the future rather than cling by our fingernails to the life we once knew. Keeping our eyes forward requires strength from a heart where the Redeemer resides.

Then there's Noah's wife. We sometimes assume she had no choice, but she had the same one Lot's wife had. Odd that we only know each of these women by their husbands' names—men who were called out from the familiar to follow the God they knew into a future made certain only by His presence there.

> **Keeping our eyes forward requires strength from a heart where the Redeemer resides.**

Men invited to bring their families.

Mrs. Noah had a choice. It seems she chose not to hold on to her life, and so she kept it. It's probably a mistake to view her as the children's board books depict her—a gentle old woman happily sweeping up after the lions.

As she watched her husband obey God's commands, Noah's wife was forced to prepare for the destruction of life as she knew it. She may have watched her neighbors and friends scoff at Noah as he labored for decades building an ark in a desert. We know he was a "herald of righteousness" (2 Peter 2:5) and yet anyone who heard him obviously continued to ignore their Creator and live sinfully, their days marked by violence and corruption. We can only guess what those years were like.

Imagine the emotional strain of wondering what was ahead. God had told Noah, "Behold, I will bring a flood of waters upon the earth to destroy all flesh in which is the breath of life under heaven. Everything that is on the earth shall die" (Genesis 6:17). It was likely a mixed blessing that the ark took many years to build. It may have given the family time to adjust to the idea, but it would have meant years of enduring speculation about the future.

No adjustment, I imagine, could minimize the trauma of being safe inside the ark when the rains came, knowing everyone else was about to be lost beneath the waters of God's judgment. Every former neighbor. Every animal not safe within the ark. Every flower or tree that Mrs. Noah might have enjoyed except what they might have saved aboard. We make movies about the end of the world as we know it. She was an eyewitness.

We can't fathom it. Flooding rains. Forty days and forty nights on a great ship full of animals, wondering what the world would be like when the waters receded. Then, knowing.

Knowing that it's on your family to start again. Looking at your sons and their wives as the magnitude of what has happened sinks in. Did the younger women need comfort? Were they afraid? Was it clear where to start? And how? Did they agree on a plan? Was there time to reflect on what was lost, or did Noah keep everyone focused on survival?

When we talk about pioneers, we never mention Noah and his wife, but who merits the title more? Of all the forward-focused women in Scripture, Mrs. Noah exemplifies those who looked ahead, because she had to look ahead. Maybe that's similar to your story. At least two of her sons and their wives kept their eyes on God and on the future they were entrusted to build. What influence did her life, and Noah's, have on them?

Conversely, Lot's wife stands not only as a pillar of salt but as a warning from Jesus not to cling to our past or to our lives as we know them. Not when God has called us forward into something new.

She and Lot lived where the people were violent, ungodly, and inhospitable. Even so, that was her home. It's often not until we escape a bad situation that we realize all we'd closed our eyes to while remaining where we were.

Lot's wife looked back. Jesus tells us it was her attempt to preserve her life.

When we turn from lives of sin to follow God, He wants our

whole hearts and attention, backed up by actions. We cannot be double minded in our devotion to Christ. It's true that in the scene described in Genesis, Lot and his family had very little time to respond to the angels' demand that they leave. But three of the family of four kept their eyes forward. Three of the family followed instructions. Only one turned back. Only one tried to preserve the life she once knew.

The gut-level decisions we make in a crisis reveal the true state of our hearts. Lot's wife revealed that part of her heart remained with the city destined for destruction and not with Lot's God.

This is a tough story. It's made tougher still by Jesus's reference to it. Our actions matter. Often for eternity.

Would Lot's daughters have made the foolish decision to become pregnant by their father if their mother had been available for counsel? Would Lot have had the courage to move to a more populated place if his wife had survived? We'll never know because that future became a pillar of salt the moment she turned back.

BIBLE

Jesus followers are called the "salt of the earth" in the New Testament, and that's a positive designation. However, the Old Testament often refers to "salt wastelands." Read these passages and consider why the decision to preserve her life resulted in Lot's wife becoming salt: Psalm 107:33–35; Jeremiah 17:6; and Deuteronomy 29:22–24.

The story of Noah's wife and her family is found in Genesis 6:9 through 9:29. Read it with adult eyes and not the eyes of a child. Don't focus on the animals. Focus on the family.

Bible Extra

A funny story in Scripture about not looking back is recorded in Acts 12:12–16 when Peter was delivered from prison by an angel. Peter went to the home of Mary, mother of John Mark. When Rhoda, the servant girl, answered the door and saw Peter, she neglected to let him in. She turned to let everyone know Peter was at the gate and didn't look back.

Unfortunately, this left Peter standing at the gate while those inside tried to convince Rhoda she'd seen Peter's angel, not Peter. Thankfully, they finally heard his banging and let poor Peter inside. There was no long-term harm from her behavior, but it's a story worth a chuckle.

BATTLE

There is a big difference between reflecting on the past to learn from it or to preserve important history versus clinging to a familiar worldly life or the comfortable status quo rather than following God into an uncertain future. Clinging to the familiar can negatively ripple across generations. It sets an ungodly example for those who come up behind us. It's not easy to let go. One key is to remember who God is all the time. Doing so fortifies our trust, resulting in the courage to have a forward view.

Bottom Line

Remember Lot's wife.

Miriam and Herodias's Daughter

The Impact of Celebration

Out of them shall come songs of thanksgiving, and the voices of those who celebrate. I will multiply them, and they shall not be few; I will make them honored, and they shall not be small.

Jeremiah 30:19

How unique to love a God who weaves regular times of celebration into the shared life of His people.

How kind that our Creator designed us to love gatherings, to enjoy delicious food, and to rejoice together with music and dance. He is a God like no other. Our lives are not all about work but they also consist of rest and joyful commemoration of significant events.

There are many examples in the Bible. When God gave Israel victory in battle, leaders led the people in song, instrumental music, and dance. God instructed His people to celebrate Passover and feasts. Ezra and Nehemiah facilitated celebrations as the Israelites reunited after the dispersion, remembered God's

Word, and honored the restoration of the wall around Jerusalem. That elaborate celebration is described in Nehemiah 12:

> At the dedication of the wall of Jerusalem they sought the Levites in all their places, to bring them to Jerusalem to celebrate the dedication with gladness, with thanksgivings and with singing, with cymbals, harps, and lyres. (v. 27)

> Then I brought the leaders of Judah up onto the wall and appointed two great choirs that gave thanks. One went to the south on the wall to the Dung Gate. . . . The other choir of those who gave thanks went to the north. (vv. 31, 38)

> The singers sang with Jezrahiah as their leader. And they offered great sacrifices that day and rejoiced, for God had made them rejoice with great joy; the women and children also rejoiced. And the joy of Jerusalem was heard far away. (vv. 42–43)

Throughout Scripture, God invites us to rejoice. When heaven and earth are made new again, we will likely continue to rejoice, but with purity of motive as well as joyful noise. Until that day, sin still creeps in and finds ways to twist this gift God gave us.

It's always wise to contemplate if we're celebrating our God, what He has done, what He has provided, and what He has designed, or if we're celebrating only ourselves. Are we including God in celebrations, or have we taken His gift of celebration and run off to spend it only on our own pleasures?

Why does this matter? Just ask John the Baptist. The prophet's death took place at a celebration.

King Herod held a banquet in honor of his own birthday and invited military leaders, nobles, and the leading men of Galilee (Mark 6:14–29). Many people enjoy celebrating birthdays. It's wonderful to thank God for another year of life. King Herod's celebration, however, took a gruesome turn.

John the Baptist was accustomed to not making friends through his message of repentance for sins. He was frank in his work and preached against Herod's illicit relationship with his brother's wife, Herodias. The outcome was as you might expect from leaders accustomed to people's blank approval. "Herodias had a grudge against him and wanted to put him to death" (v. 19).

Herod had a more complicated reaction to John. "Herod feared John, knowing that he was a righteous and holy man, and he kept him safe. When he heard him, he was greatly perplexed, and yet he heard him gladly" (v. 20).

Interesting to see back then what we see still in our times. Some readily accept prophecies and teachings about Jesus. Others definitively reject them. But still others experience conflicted reactions and may be influenced in either direction.

Anyway, while John sat in jail for his words, Herod threw himself a party.

At the festivities, Herodias's daughter danced for the guests. She isn't named in the Bible, but the ancient historian Josephus identifies her as Salome.[5] Her dance pleased Herod and his guests, so he promised her anything she asked of him, up to half of his kingdom.

Salome had a choice. This was a gala. A day to rejoice. The decision she made turned it into a macabre spectacle.

We have no idea what *she* wanted because she requested of the king what her mother desired—John's head on a plate, immediately.

What was happening behind the scenes? There's evidence of fear woven throughout this story. Clues to hidden power.

You'd think a young woman would optimize this rare opportunity and ask for what *she* most desired. Instead, she consulted her mother: "'For what should I ask?' And she [Herodias] said, 'The head of John the Baptist'" (Mark 6:24).

What was their dynamic? Devotion or fear? Was this daughterly loyalty or the machinations of a controlling parent? Was Salome truly this selfless or had they struck an earlier deal where Herodias promised her reward? Or was Herodias threatening enough that Salome could see no other option? We don't really know what motivated her to make her mother's horrifying request.

Apparently Herod harbored petty fears. You'd think a king would have the ultimate say in his kingdom, especially on his birthday. But Herod feared going back on his word—looking weak—in front of his gathering. At Salome's request, "the king was exceedingly sorry, but because of his oaths and his guests he did not want to break his word to her" (Mark 6:26).

Herodias clearly feared no one—almost. We can surmise that she feared John's Holy Spirit–fueled preaching because she was willing to trade her daughter's financial future to silence it.

What was the outcome of the decision? An undignified death for an anointed prophet. John's death highlighted that people can love their sin so much they become twisted toward evil. Even a party can morph into an execution when people choose to celebrate only themselves.

We use the phrase "dance with the devil" to signify when someone engages in reckless behavior that leads to unfortunate consequences. Salome's dance was simply a dance. Her unwise decision to honor her mother's wishes and request John the Baptist's head was her true *pas de deux* with the devil.

Conversely, celebration can be joyful *and* honor God.

The Israelites escaped death through God's deliverance from Egypt. "When Pharaoh let the people go, God did not lead them by way of the land of the Philistines, although that was near. For God said, 'Lest the people change their minds when they see war and return to Egypt.' But God led the people around by the way of the wilderness toward the Red Sea. And the people of Israel went up out of the land of Egypt equipped for battle" (Exodus 13:17–18).

The last line indicates that the Israelites believed they were ready for battle. God knew otherwise. Conversely, they knew immediately they weren't prepared to face the Red Sea! Sometimes, when we face the unexpected, we should consider the possibility that we've been spared from a worse option for which we are even less prepared. God glorified himself by parting the waters, allowing the children of Israel to cross safely. When Pharaoh's army pursued them, the waters closed over them.

Delivered from slavery! Miraculously led through the impassable sea and saved from the mightiest army on earth, the Israelites were ready to celebrate. They didn't celebrate themselves, though. Instead, Moses and Miriam led them in a song with music and dancing to celebrate God and all He had done.

By God's providence, Moses had been saved from the waters in his infancy, with Miriam looking on. Now, all the people of God were saved through the waters as Moses, Aaron, and Miriam witnessed God's deliverance. This foreshadowed baptism, which symbolizes dying to self and rising again to live for Christ.

In everything, we don't celebrate just us but the work of Jesus in and through our lives. While Salome's influence highlights the dark side of celebrations where focus strays from Christ-centered to self-centered, the graceful influence of Israel's celebration is a model of giving God glory in triumph.

> **Maintaining a focus on God isn't about being somber. We can let loose at celebrations without letting go of what's right, loving, and true.**

People should celebrate often and receive celebration as one of God's gifts to enjoy. Maintaining a focus on God isn't about being somber all the time or praying at parties instead of playing music and dancing. It's about remembering God is present. We can let loose at celebrations without letting go of what's right, loving, and true.

Jesus blessed celebrations. The gospel of John records Jesus attending the wedding at Cana (John 2:1–12) and several times eating as a guest of both "sinners" and Pharisees. He even states that some falsely accused Him of attending too many parties. "The Son of Man came eating and drinking, and they say, 'Look at him! A glutton and a drunkard, a friend of tax collectors and sinners!' Yet wisdom is justified by her deeds" (Matthew 11:19).

Many of His parables regarding the kingdom of heaven feature great feasts or celebrations. The story of the prodigal son, in fact, concludes with the father pleading with the older brother to join the party. The angel in Revelation told John, "Write this: Blessed are those who are invited to the marriage supper of the Lamb" (Revelation 19:9). Jesus encourages gathering, but gathering that is centered on life in Him.

When we focus on ourselves or seek to silence God in our lives, we set the stage for celebrations that may revel in the dark side of humanity. When we celebrate remembering the author of our salvation, our celebrations can be full of life.

BIBLE

Read Exodus 15:1–21. Consider the powerful use of language in celebrating God and what He's done. The celebration appears to have been spontaneous, yet rich poetry was used to proclaim God's glorious act.

Bible Extra

Read Nehemiah 12:27–47. Consider the detail involved in arranging that celebration. Look at the value placed on the musicians. They were supported like the Levites were. What does this tell us about the priority of celebrating God and what He's done?

BATTLE

There is battle around celebration because our enemy wants to rob the joy we have in the Lord. He knows it is our strength. To choose to celebrate God regularly is to choose a life marked by moments of joy. When we neglect celebrations, we go through long solemn times and leave ourselves at risk of losing heart.

So our first battle is to choose to celebrate regularly. Our second battle is to celebrate God over celebrating self. That doesn't mean we don't celebrate individuals, but we celebrate them in the context of God's work in and through their lives so we don't risk losing perspective.

Bottom Line

To celebrate often is to access the joy of
the Lord, which is our strength.

16

Wailing Women and Laughing Women

The Impact of Lament

*Thus says the LORD of hosts: "Consider, and call for the
mourning women to come; send for the skillful women to come;
let them make haste and raise a wailing over us, that our eyes
may run down with tears and our eyelids flow with water."*

Jeremiah 9:17–18

In the 1987 romantic comedy *Broadcast News*, Holly Hunter played an ambitious news producer. When we meet her, she's weeping. She's not sad. She schedules daily crying time in the belief that if she stores up all her negative feelings for one short, controlled episode, she won't come unglued at work.

Later, she realizes her folly when her coworker, a reporter, cries on cue to enhance his interview. She acknowledges the risk that shutting off certain emotions can lead to shutting off all emotions. While Hunter's character missed the mark, she wasn't totally off track. We do need to create space in our lives for sadness and lament.

Inside Out, released in 2015 by Pixar, portrayed the importance of respecting our emotional design. Eleven-year-old Riley has a hard time adjusting to her family's cross-country move. Her personified emotions, especially Joy, try to help Riley by blocking Sadness. Joy will learn, though, that Riley needs Sadness to process change and reengage with life.

In ancient Israel, as in many ancient cultures, there were professional mourners, usually women. When a family experienced a loss, they would call the mourners to weep, wail, tear at their hair and clothing, and walk in the funeral processional.

The wealthier and more important the dead person, the greater the number of mourners and hence the greater display of grief. While some family members might also openly express their sorrow, many took the opportunity to maintain their emotional dignity in public, relying solely on the paid mourners to demonstrate the magnitude of their loss. They effectively outsourced their grief.

Sometimes Christians too wander from God's design by thinking our joy in Christ means we shouldn't express sadness or grief. Maybe we think those emotions merit a brief visit, but nothing prolonged, certainly. We stifle or rush through unpleasant feelings, sometimes out of shame, sometimes with good intention, and often driven by pressure from others who just want us to heal and move on.

> **We all benefit from trusting that God knew what He was doing when He created us with a range of feelings.**

Christians from some cultures do better at respecting lament than others, but we all benefit from trusting that God knew what He was doing when He created us with a range of feelings. Jesus had feelings. He wept at Lazarus's death and was "a man of sorrows and acquainted with grief" (Isaiah 53:3). As painful as it is to experience and express great sadness, too often the alternative is to become callous or cynical about sin, loss, and death.

When Jeremiah was a prophet of Israel, the people had grown emotionally hard. They were so unfeeling God told Jeremiah to call in the professional mourning women (Jeremiah 9:17–18). The Israelites weren't responding to the prophet's messages with repentance and sorrow over their sin, so God told Jeremiah to instruct the women who mourn to weep and wail over His people. More than that, He wanted the mothers to instruct their daughters to lament and teach their neighbors a dirge so the people could recover the language of lament.

We suppress or deny our grief at the price of our hearts. When our hearts petrify because of sin, they harden also to God. We are no longer moved or softened by life. Every time we choose not to let sorrow touch us or to lament over sin or loss, we distance ourselves from our humanity.

The weeping women were called on to recover the pathway to our full experience of what it means to be human under God. Their graceful influence reminds us there is currently a place for sadness and lament, particularly in repentance.

When Jesus came, He found hardness of heart—a people grown callous toward death. This side of glory, we may resolve ourselves to the inevitability of death, but if we grow numb to it, celebrate it (as some extremists do), or view it cynically, we can lose touch with our souls.

My father, a career fire chief, trained firefighters to respect victims, no matter the pain of witnessing suffering and death. Put the patient first. He never allowed joking about accident or rescue victims out of respect for human life—both theirs and his firefighters'. It's more challenging to face head-on the human element of each loss or tragedy but hardness in that area never stays contained. It seeps into other areas of a person's mindset until they become unfeeling toward even what is beautiful and happy in life.

When Jesus arrived at Jairus's house, He found many mourners, most likely the professional weeping women, crying for Jairus's daughter (Luke 8:41–42, 51–52). When He told them to stop crying because she was only asleep, "they laughed at him, knowing that she was dead" (Luke 8:53). They knew what they knew. The word used for laughter here is often translated "laughed him to scorn" or "ridiculed," indicating a stony laughter, not merely surprise that Jesus could be so naive. Knowing death as we do, we might also have scorned.

But perhaps, if our hearts were open to God, we might simply go quiet and wait to see what God would do. The mourners likely knew the stories from Elijah about the dead rising and Ezekiel's prophecy that God can breathe life into dead bones. But trusting those stories requires faith. The professional wailing women here are not unlike Hunter's coworker in *Broadcast News*. They turned their tears on and off.

To lament, truly lament, is to acknowledge our fragility and the toll that sin, sorrow, and death take on our hearts. Choosing to honor the full range of our emotions and the full experience of living in a broken, hurting world is not easy, but it moves us toward our need for Jesus. It reminds us how far we are from what He created and how desperately we need saving. It requires us to lean on the armor He provides rather than the armor we create through petrifying our hearts or denying our emotions.

Jesus lamented over Jerusalem: "O Jerusalem, Jerusalem, the city that kills the prophets and stones those who are sent to it! How often would I have gathered your children together as a hen gathers her brood under her wings, and you were not willing! See, your house is left to you desolate. For I tell you, you will not see me again, until you say, 'Blessed is he who comes in the name of the Lord'" (Matthew 23:37–39).

Israel had experienced a hardening of heart and incurred God's anger (Ezekiel 3:7; Zechariah 7:11–13). While, no doubt, there were individuals who expressed true sadness and grief, as a culture, they were losing the heart of lament. But at the coming of Christ, we see some hearts softened and genuine tears flowing.

The birth of Jesus was bathed in tears when Herod ordered the murder of all boys under two. "A voice was heard in Ramah, weeping and loud lamentation, Rachel weeping for her children; she refused to be comforted, because they are no more" (Matthew 2:18).

Women wept again at Jesus's death. As He walked toward crucifixion, "there followed him a great multitude of the people and of women who were mourning and lamenting for him" (Luke 23:27). Jesus told them not to weep for Him but for themselves and their children. His ministry had helped them soften and rediscover the language of lament. Now He guided them to lament at what was truly sad—not His death, which would result in life, but their own lives trapped in sin, destined for eternal death.

After His resurrection, at the empty tomb, Mary Magdalene wept when she encountered the risen Christ. Her tears were genuine because her grief at the loss of the Savior was real. The graceful influence of these women who shed tears around the birth, death, and resurrection of Jesus is a sign that His ministry did exactly what Ezekiel prophesied: "And I will give you a new heart, and a new spirit I will put within you. And I will remove the heart of stone from your flesh and give you a heart of flesh" (Ezekiel 36:26).

Admittedly, when stone hearts become flesh, that means they're more likely to experience pain. But without true sorrow, they also become immune to joy.

The women around Jesus chose to lament. Rather than petrify their hearts at His coming, they opened their hearts to Him. Yes, this meant recovering their expression of grief in the now—but when Jesus comes again, all mourning will cease (Revelation 21:4).

BIBLE

Read John 16:19–21. What is Jesus saying about the transient nature of lament? What is the purpose of lament in this time before the second coming of Jesus? How can sorrow and grief in the face of sin or death be cathartic or a benefit in healing?

In Lamentations 3, Jeremiah flows from lament into hope. How does his lament facilitate hope?

Why will we have no need for lament in the new heaven and earth (Revelation 21:1–4)?

Bible Extra

During King David's reign, Israel experienced a three-year famine (2 Samuel 21:1–14). When David asked God why, God told him there was bloodguilt on the house of Saul regarding the Gibeonites. The Gibeonites said that to atone for Saul, they demanded to hang seven of Saul's sons. King David agreed. It's not hard to understand that leaders of nations who had seen death in battle or by famine might be callous to the loss of seven lives that would make everything square between the nations.

Rizpah, the mother of two of those sons who died, was not of the same heart. "Rizpah the daughter of Aiah took sackcloth and spread it for herself on the rock, from the beginning of harvest until rain fell upon them from the heavens. And she did not allow the birds of the air to come upon them by day, or the beasts of the field by night" (2 Samuel 21:10).

Is there a more poignant image of lamentation? Rizpah's actions moved David to gather the bones of those hanged and bury them with Saul and Jonathan. We can only imagine that her expression of lament may have served to remind him to soften his heart, even in the hard business of leadership and battle.

BATTLE

Christians live with great hope for the kingdom that is "now and not yet." Jesus has won the victory over Satan and death, but we do not yet see this victory reflected in all of life. Our life now is informed by the tension of living with the hope of heaven that brings us joy but also the reality that sin, loss, pain, and death will be evident until He comes again. Petrifying our hearts is ineffective self-protection. Choosing to lament and acknowledge the pain of what sin causes honors our humanity and reminds us of our need for Christ.

Bottom Line

When Jesus comes again, all mourning
will cease. Until then, faith makes
room for honest, healing lament.

17

Orpah and Mary Magdalene

The Impact of Following

After this many of his disciples turned back and no longer walked with him. So Jesus said to the twelve, "Do you want to go away as well?"

John 6:66–67

When I was in college, the small group leader at my church was one determined Christian. He led our group every week, taught a class at church, did one-on-one discipling, and witnessed at work.

Ten years later, I learned he had walked away from his wife, young children, and Jesus. One day he was following Jesus; the next, he was following his own desires.

In the Gospels, there were some who initially appeared to follow Jesus. They responded positively to His teaching, witnessed healings and miracles, formed part of the crowd around Him, but eventually walked away. The rich young ruler. Those disciples mentioned in John 6. Judas.

Jesus told a parable about seed that fell along the path and was immediately eaten by birds. Other seed fell on rocky soil, at first springing up but then getting scorched by the sun. Still other seed fell among thorns and eventually got choked out. But some seed fell on good soil and produced good grain (Matthew 13:1–9).

Jesus explained that this parable described some who would never receive the Word planted in them; some who would hear, but persecution or trial would send them away; and others who would also hear, but worldly riches and cares would turn them back. However, a few who received the Word would bear good fruit (vv. 18–23). Jesus knew that not everyone who met Him or heard Him teach would follow Him. Some would turn back from following.

Many of us know people who started out walking beside us in our faith. Perhaps they attended youth group or church camp with us. They were on fire for the gospel or active in church, but as they aged, they walked away. Other times we've seen even church leaders, who appeared so firm in their faith, face a devastating event or persecution that shook them off the foundation of their relationship with God.

It's almost become a trend for celebrity Christians to announce they're walking away from Jesus and explain, in detail, what caused their disillusionment. Sometimes they cite church conflict. Other times it's personal situations. Some, discouraged by hypocrisy or scandal in the church, lose faith that following Jesus makes a difference. So they stop.

There are people who turn away suddenly or dramatically. But Jesus followers who slowly drift away—"quiet quitters" who continue to fill the pews while spiritually disengaging from the faith—also affect us. Every time someone we know, love, or admire walks away from Jesus, there's an impact. We hurt. We question. We wonder.

In the book of Ruth, two daughters-in-law, Orpah and Ruth, had an opportunity to turn back from following the God of the family into which they married. Their mother-in-law,

Naomi, and her husband, Elimelech, had left Israel and traveled to Moab to escape a famine. There, they married their sons, Mahlon and Kilion, to these Moabite women. The couples were married for ten years when both sons died. Naomi herself had already been widowed, and the loss of her sons created bitterness in her spirit.

Naomi heard God had once again provided food in Israel, so she and her two daughters-in-law started back toward the homeland of her people and her God. But after a short time, Naomi turned to the young widows and encouraged them to turn around (Ruth 1:6–9).

It seemed a reasonable encouragement. Naomi indicated that she had no other sons to provide for the women, so they should return to their tribe and hope for new husbands. Initially, both women protested and insisted they would not turn around. They would continue to follow Naomi to Israel.

Naomi insisted. She pushed both women. She had allowed bitterness to twist her heart, and this may have influenced her understanding of God's provision. Perhaps her faith was wavering, with the potential to diminish her confidence that God would provide for these two young widows. So she insisted they turn back.

At last, Orpah did.

Here's the thing about Orpah's decision. It seems logical. There is a worldly wisdom about not moving forward to follow Naomi and her God. Besides the usual crying involved in a goodbye that will likely be permanent, the situation is not even dramatic. Looking on from the outside, we're almost unmoved by Orpah's turning around to return home.

We understand why she walked away from Naomi, but we miss that she's also turning back from following her husband's and mother-in-law's God. "Orpah kissed her mother-in-law, but Ruth clung to her. And [Naomi] said, 'See, your sister-in-law has gone back to her people and to her gods; return after your sister-in-law'" (Ruth 1:14–15).

Orpah stopped following; Ruth insisted on forging on. She influenced future generations for the kingdom, but Orpah's story ends here.

The decision to follow Jesus isn't an easy one. It certainly wasn't easy for any of the first followers. Mary Magdalene, though, was and still is known for her devotion to following Jesus.

For all the legends and stories that have built up around Mary Magdalene, the truth is we know very little about her apart from her love of Jesus. She's mentioned only about twelve times in the Bible, mostly in association with the burial and resurrection of Jesus.

While she has become associated with "sinful" women, all we really know of Mary's past is detailed in Luke 8:1–3: "The twelve were with him, and also some women who had been healed of evil spirits and infirmities: Mary, called Magdalene, from whom seven demons had gone out, and Joanna, the wife of Chuza, Herod's household manager, and Susanna, and many others, who provided for them out of their means."

From this, we learn Mary was delivered from demons. How these demons affected her physical and mental health, we don't know. How she fell prey to them, we don't know. What we do know is that she followed Jesus, providing for Him out of her means along with other women followers.

Mary Magdalene stood by the cross (John 19:25) and sat opposite the tomb when the stone was rolled across the entrance (Matthew 27:61). She went to the tomb early with the other women to anoint His body with spices, and these women were the first to find the empty tomb, which they reported to the disciples (Luke 24:1–10).

Finally, John describes a beautiful moment between the risen Christ and Mary in the garden, where she was weeping and wondering where He'd been taken (John 20:11–18). Mary didn't recognize Jesus until He spoke her name. He warned her not to cling to Him as He hadn't yet ascended to the Father.

Then He sent her to tell the apostles what she had seen, and she bore witness to them as the first follower to see Jesus alive from the dead.

What we know for certain about Mary Magdalene is that she loved and followed Jesus. Jesus set her free, and so she followed Him. Mary, like us, would have had opportunities to turn away, such as the incident in John 6:66, when many disciples left him. Mary remained. She was at the cross, she was at the tomb, and she was the first eyewitness to His resurrection. Mary announced to the apostles, "I have seen the Lord" (John 20:18).

That Mary and the other women followed Jesus is significant. Women were welcomed into Jesus's inner circle, and despite the intensity of His arrest, trial, and crucifixion, women like Mary followed Him to the end and beyond. He can strengthen us all, male and female, to follow Him in the same manner. He frees us, and if we follow Him, He empowers us to do so.

> **Women were welcomed into Jesus's inner circle, and despite the intensity of His arrest, trial, and crucifixion, women like Mary followed Him to the end and beyond.**

With all the other messages we try to create around Mary Magdalene, I believe her simple, graceful impact is to remind us of the power of following Jesus. Even when it becomes challenging, following Him not only makes our lives worthwhile, but it also encourages others to not turn back. Daily, like her, we choose to follow.

BIBLE

We understand Orpah because there is nothing more naturally human than returning home to the familiarity of our family. But

Jesus calls us to follow Him and to place all human relationships beneath our allegiance to Him.

Read Matthew 10:34–38. Prayerfully consider what following Jesus looks like in your life. Are you still, like Mary Magdalene, following Him through everything, or are there quiet ways you've turned back to what is old and familiar?

Bible Extra

Read Hebrews 11:8–16. What were those who lived by faith looking toward? What difference did that make in their decision-making? Whom were they following in faith?

BATTLE

Just as the ocean tide exerts a constant pull to drag us down the beach, so the world is relentless in attempting to drag us from following Jesus. Sometimes its pull is dramatic and obvious, but more often, as with Orpah, it is quiet, subtle, and makes a kind of worldly sense. Like Mary Magdalene, we must cultivate grateful, loving hearts that follow Jesus through every trial, knowing He is worthy always.

The battle to follow Jesus differs through the ages and across cultures. To the early disciples, following Jesus meant to risk imprisonment and possibly their lives. It still means that in some parts of the world today. How can we prayerfully support believers who follow Jesus in places where being a Christian might cost them everything? What are some ways we can encourage one another not to become a casualty of "drift"?

Bottom Line

Women were welcomed into Jesus's inner circle, and despite the intensity of His arrest, trial, and crucifixion, women like Mary followed Him to the end and beyond.

18

Tamar and the Adulterous Woman

The Impact of Accountability

We know that whatever the law says it speaks to those who are under the law, so that every mouth may be stopped, and the whole world may be held accountable to God. For by works of the law no human being will be justified in his sight, since through the law comes knowledge of sin.

Romans 3:19–20

Women often get a raw deal in this broken world. Throughout history and across cultures, we're stereotyped, objectified, oppressed, victimized, grievously wronged, and abused. The Bible doesn't shy away from recording specific episodes of crimes and injustices against women in the history of the Israelites.

These stories are often delivered in narrative and without commentary, as is most of the Old Testament history. Because of this, some accuse Christians of condoning the incidents or take offense that the text remains silent when it should condemn.

But when we read the Bible as a whole, we find a pattern of

teaching that promotes all people as created and loved by God. Biblical writing condemns violence, selfishness, sexual sin, abuse, greed, and unkindness. God instructs us to keep our promises, including those we make in marriage. God commands us to love one another, and all His directions on how to do this preclude the idea that He condones mistreatment of women or any other human being.

He is, however, unflinching in including even the ugly truths in the story of humanity recorded in His Word. He's meticulous about not airbrushing the men and women through whom He worked; instead, He demonstrates through imperfect people that He is clearly at work.

As a young woman, I was given charge of a church school class of third graders. I felt at the time that the stories of men in the Bible were elevated over those of women in teaching children. I was going to correct that.

I was truly humbled when I realized how the complexity of relationships as well as details of reproduction must often be explained when telling the *whole* story, especially when adding the women. It was much more than third graders could understand or than I was adept at teaching on their level.

But then, these aren't children's stories recorded to teach neat moral lessons. They are the sweeping historical narrative by which God demonstrates His plan of redemption. The biblical accounts are facts, not fables.

Tamar is a distant ancestor of Jesus (Matthew 1:3). The mention of Tamar, Rahab, Bathsheba, Ruth, and Mary in that genealogy is a strong argument that the Gospels were not devised by men but by God. Each woman's story has a social element that makes her inclusion too complicated for it to be fiction. God, however, doesn't shy away from complications.

Tamar was married to the eldest son of Judah. The fourth of Jacob's twelve sons, Judah was destined to beget the line from which the Messiah would be born. He had three sons, Er, Onan, and Shelah. Judah arranged a marriage between Tamar and Er, but Er was "wicked in the sight of the LORD, and the LORD put him to death" (Genesis 38:7).

Tamar had a right to a child, according to custom in that culture, so she would not be left desolate. So Judah instructed Onan to provide Tamar with a child who would legally be Er's offspring. Onan lay with Tamar but then ensured she wouldn't become pregnant, essentially using her body and then denying her a child (v. 9). God saw this evil and took Onan's life.

Judah was afraid now for his remaining son, Shelah's, life, so he hesitated to commit Shelah to Tamar. Instead, he requested that Tamar wait until Shelah was grown, and then he would fulfill his duty. So Tamar stayed at her father's house and waited for Judah to make good on his promise (v. 11).

After Shelah was well into his adulthood and Judah hadn't fulfilled his promise, Tamar took matters into her own hands. When Judah went to Timnah for sheep-shearing time, Tamar disguised herself as a prostitute. Judah took the bait. He promised her a goat in exchange for sex, and as security for the goat, she asked him to leave with her his signet, cord, and staff. She conceived a child but kept his belongings and returned to her home. When Judah's servant couldn't find the "prostitute" to exchange the goat, Judah let it go so he wouldn't become a laughingstock.

Three months later, word reached Judah that Tamar was pregnant, and he assumed immorality. He ordered her to be brought out and burned (v. 24). As she was brought out, she sent the belongings to Judah saying the child belonged to the owner of the signet, cord, and staff. She held Judah accountable for his neglect, and Judah's response was to acknowledge that she was in the right and he in the wrong. "She is more righteous than I, since I did not give her to my son Shelah" (v. 26). Tamar gave birth to twins, Perez and Zerah. Perez is in the line of the Messiah.

This is a complex story involving ancient customs that are challenging for modern readers to accept. What is easy to miss in the strangeness of the circumstances is that a powerless young woman chose to hold her powerful father-in-law accountable for his actions. The father-in-law accepted responsibility for this wrongdoing. Tamar's legacy is that she was not only included in the line of Jesus, but she is mentioned by name in Matthew's genealogy.

Accountability is a challenging but pivotal choice.

John is the only gospel writer to record the incident of a woman caught in adultery (John 8:1–11). Every modern Bible includes a note that the story doesn't appear in the earliest manuscripts, so I will note that here as well. What is also notable, though, is that the text describes a scene where the religious leaders brought a woman accused of adultery before Jesus—*alone*. The very nature of the sin she was accused of committing indicates there was a man involved who also should have been brought to account, but this woman stood by herself before the crowd.

It was a test, of course. The religious leaders were trying to trip Jesus up. They demanded the woman be stoned in accordance with Moses's law, and they asked Jesus what He had to say. Jesus spent moments writing with His finger in the sand before standing and announcing, "Let him who is without sin among you be the first to throw a stone at her" (v. 7). Then He returned to His writing in the sand.

One by one, the men walked away until only Jesus and the woman were left. "Jesus stood up and said to her, 'Woman, where are they? Has no one condemned you?' She said, 'No one, Lord.' And Jesus said, 'Neither do I condemn you; go, and from now on sin no more'" (vv. 10–11).

The man who had committed adultery with her did not accept responsibility, and no person there held him accountable. The two had been "caught," so of course others knew his identity. Yet they remained silent.

They all left the woman alone at Jesus's mercy, which she received, along with the instruction to sin no more. Jesus didn't let her off the hook. He knew He was about to offer His own life for every sin she and each man in the crowd had committed. He held the entire crowd accountable for the truth that not one of them could claim to be without sin.

What is clear in both these stories is that some people have power while others are powerless, but all sin and are accountable to God.

Tamar called Judah to account, and Jesus called the crowd to account. Jesus is the only one with an answer for all these sins. His death and resurrection resulted in grace and forgiveness for all who come to Him.

In the second story, the outcome of the lack of accountability for sin was great corporate shame. Unconfessed, unaddressed sin lingered like a foreboding cloud as, one by one, each man walked away from Jesus. In the first story, when Tamar called Judah to account for his sin, he accepted the opportunity to take responsibility. He and Tamar could then move forward. In John's story, only the woman was able to walk forward free of shame because she received mercy from Jesus.

The choice to hold one another accountable for sin is not about exercising a judgmental attitude; it's about opening a pathway out of shame and into healing. No one in these stories was without sin except Jesus. And isn't that the truth at the heart of the gospel?

> **The choice to hold one another accountable for sin is not about exercising a judgmental attitude; it's about opening a pathway out of shame and into healing.**

BIBLE

God called David to account for arranging for the death of Bathsheba's husband, Uriah, following David's adultery with

Bathsheba. Read how Nathan the prophet confronted David in 2 Samuel 12:1–13 and read David's response in Psalm 51.

The Bible offers guidance about how to confront someone in sin and hold them accountable in passages such as Matthew 18:15; Galatians 6:1; and 1 Timothy 5:20. Like Nathan, we can be prayerfully instrumental in leading brothers and sisters into repentance and/or accountability for their sins.

Bible Extra

There are other difficult narratives in Israel's history where women were hurt because the people ignored God's command not to intermarry or engage in idolatry with pagans. Numbers 25 tells the story of Cozbi, a Midianite woman who was killed in her adultery with an Israelite. Ezra 10 records Israelite leaders commanding husbands to send away foreign wives and children born in disobedience. In both cases, if accountability had come sooner, the devastation wouldn't have been so severe. Keeping short accounts with God leads not only to greater blessing for those who obey but reduced fallout and pain for those affected by the sins of others.

BATTLE

There's an element of discomfort in holding people accountable for their actions, particularly those that occur in intimate settings. Loving but frank confrontation can be a complex and delicate process that requires sensitivity but also a persistent commitment to seeking truth. Sadly, however, when people are not called to account, the suffering of their victims can be long lasting and can sometimes drive them, and others, away from God.

It's easier for any of us to look the other way or hope that a problem isn't as bad as it first appears. Unfortunately, even within the church we must call people to account for their sometimes grievous sins against others. The choice to seek accountability, and to be held accountable, results in helping validate victims' needs and providing them help sooner rather than later. Holding others accountable for their actions also strengthens confidence in the fairness and justice of God, which encourages faith.

Bottom Line

Holding one another accountable for sin is not about exercising a judgmental attitude; it's about opening a pathway out of shame and into healing.

Mother Zebedee and the Syrophoenician Mother

The Impact of Humility

Humble yourselves before the Lord, and he will exalt you.

James 4:10

Mothers want the best for their children. Even those who mother other people's children or simply care about children want the best for them. That's a global sentiment (though in a fallen world, there are certainly individual exceptions). Most of us want the best for children; it's knowing what that "best" is that requires wisdom.

I thought I had faith until I had children. It was one thing to trust God with my future, but to hold my newborn and consider all the world offers of danger, sin, and hard times—that required a whole new level of faith.

As they grew, of course I thought my children were worthy of the best, even when they weren't. As the mother of humans, I want them to be healthy and happy and to live without want. As a mother who follows Jesus, I want them to be in relationship with Him, to love Him and obey His Word, and to be at work in the kingdom. You know, that's all. No pressure.

We refer to our children as our pride and joy. It has been reported that King George VI used that phrase regarding his two daughters, as in, "Lilibet is my pride. Margaret is my joy." We can be tripped up either by pride or by seeking joy from our children instead of from God.

Two New Testament mothers approached Jesus on behalf of their children. We can imagine they too wanted what was best for them. One, a Jewish woman known well to Jesus, walked away without what she requested. The second, a stranger to Jesus and a Syrophoenician, received her request. The distinguishing element between the stories is humility.

The first mother had two sons. There are many things to adore about James and John, the "Boanerges," or "Sons of Thunder" (Mark 3:17). Jesus loved them and included them, along with Peter, in His innermost circle. We don't know why Jesus chose that nickname for the brothers, but in Luke 9:51–56, when a Samaritan town would not receive Jesus, the pair offered to call down fire from heaven to consume it. This impulsive and aggressive offer earned them a rebuke. Could be their volatile nature contributed to the Boanerges moniker.

They were, however, committed to Jesus. James was the first apostle to die (Acts 12:2), and John the last, following his exile on Patmos. They were the sons of Zebedee, a fisherman, and his wife. We'll call her Mother Zebedee.

On one occasion, Mother Zebedee brought her two sons with her and knelt before Jesus. That is certainly the posture of humility. Then, she made her request. She asked that her sons might sit, one at Jesus's left hand and one at His right, when He came into His kingdom. You know, that's all (Matthew 20:20–21).

Jesus didn't scold her or throw her sons off the team of apostles for this clearly prideful request. James and John were beside her, and each assured Jesus they were capable of this honor.

Still, He didn't grant what she'd asked because (a) He knew she didn't know what she was asking; (b) He knew she was probably thinking of an earthly kingdom like everyone else; and (c) it was not His to grant but the Father's alone (vv. 22–23).

Now, while Jesus didn't respond with anger, the other apostles were not as calm when they heard what happened. They were indignant! I'm sure there were a lot of "Who do you think you are?" asked of the brothers. Jesus called the disciples to Him and told them that whoever wanted to be greatest among them must serve his brothers, not lord it over them like those who don't know God, "even as the Son of Man came not to be served but to serve, and to give his life as a ransom for many" (vv. 24–28).

Clearly, it is not simply the outward posture of humility God seeks but humility of heart. "The LORD sees not as man sees: man looks on the outward appearance, but the LORD looks on the heart" (1 Samuel 16:7).

Jesus is also humble of heart (Matthew 11:29), as Paul explains in greater detail:

> Do nothing from selfish ambition or conceit, but in humility count others more significant than yourselves. Let each of you look not only to his own interests, but also to the interests of others. Have this mind among yourselves, which is yours in Christ Jesus, who, though he was in the form of God, did not count equality with God a thing to be grasped, but emptied himself, by taking the form of a servant, being born in the likeness of men. And being found in human form, he humbled himself by becoming obedient to the point of death, even death on a cross. (Philippians 2:3–8)

It's natural in this sinful world that we, the pinnacle of creation, would be tempted to pride. But Jesus set the example of humility with His own life and gives us, by the power of His

Holy Spirit, the ability to cultivate humility. If the Creator of the universe can walk beside His creations in humility, we surely owe Him no less.

Which brings us to our other mother.

When Jesus was in Tyre and Sidon, He tried to remain hidden, but of course word of His coming spread (Mark 7:24–25). A Gentile woman, a Syrophoenician, likely from the territory of Syria, "begged him to cast [a] demon out of her daughter" (v. 26).

Jesus pushed back against her request, challenging her with words that sound harsh to modern ears. He suggested that since she was not a Jew, she was asking that bread be taken from His children and thrown to her, a Gentile. "But she answered him, 'Yes, Lord; yet even the dogs under the table eat the children's crumbs.' And he said to her, 'For this statement you may go your way; the demon has left your daughter.' And she went home and found the child lying in bed and the demon gone" (vv. 27–30).

Her response demonstrated humility of heart and faith in Jesus's power. His answer was to commend her and deliver her child.

What is captured in the humility of this mother's words is her understanding that she is completely dependent on Jesus. She makes no claim except on His goodness, which He then demonstrates in response.

Her decision to forget about herself, humble herself completely, and demonstrate confidence in Christ alone, led to her daughter's freedom. The exchange also provides us with a challenging portion of Scripture with which to wrestle and an example of humility that is relevant even today.

To modern ears, the words used by Jesus and the woman are harsh. They reflect a humility we're uncomfortable witnessing in our day. We want to look away from this moment. We rankle, rightly, at the notion that one's nationality, religion, or social status would exclude any person from what Jesus came to bring. And yet, we have Jesus to thank that we now see life this way (Galatians 3:28).

His coming changed everything. It introduced the world to the idea that in Jesus, we all are equally sinful and equally able to receive salvation. The exchange between Jesus and the woman foreshadows that the redemption He came to provide would be for all people.

> **We benefit from prayerfully examining our discomfort.**

We benefit from prayerfully examining our discomfort with the Syrophoenician woman. Many of us must admit we can identify with James and John's mother, but we resist identifying with this woman whose petition for her child was answered.

Her humility stems from a right understanding of Jesus's power, while her boldness stems from a right understanding of His goodness.

BIBLE

This chapter was about two women, one who chose humility and one who didn't. Jesus told a parable about two men: one proud, one humble. Read Luke 18:9–14. Consider what it looks like in your life to humble yourself. What helps facilitate humility in your life, and what can tempt you to pride?

Reflect on Philippians 2:1–18, considering Jesus's example of humility and the influence of Christlike humility in His followers.

Bible Extra

Many know the story of Samson, who was far from an example of humility; lesser known is the story of his father, Manoah, and Manoah's wife. Judges chapter 13 describes their prayers for a child and the angelic visitor who informed them their prayer was answered. The humility Manoah and his wife displayed toward their visitor, toward one another, and toward God can be a graceful influence on us all.

BATTLE

We live in times of confusing messages about pride and humility. God certainly doesn't want women to put themselves down or suffer the negative effects of a poor self-image, but there's a difference between humility and low self-esteem. There's also a difference between self-confidence and arrogance. Pride and low self-esteem have in common an over-focus on self. Humble people who carry themselves with confidence generally have a healthy enough view of themselves to be free to focus on others.

Paul warned Timothy that in the last days "people will be lovers of self, lovers of money, proud, arrogant, abusive, disobedient to their parents, ungrateful, unholy, heartless, unappeasable, slanderous, without self-control, brutal, not loving good, treacherous, reckless, swollen with conceit, lovers of pleasure rather than lovers of God" (2 Timothy 3:2–4).

Not only is it one of our central battles to worship God and not ourselves, but much of the messaging in our modern society feeds the lie that we deserve to nurture pride. Humility isn't celebrated, and too often it's mocked or knocked as unhealthy.

It is truly countercultural to live by the "gentle and lowly in heart" character of Christ (Matthew 11:29). In these days of divisiveness, the good messages of having healthy self-respect and honoring individual cultures can easily be twisted to honor only pride. We must support one another in developing humble hearts.

Bottom Line

Humility stems from a right understanding
of Jesus's position, while boldness stems from
a right understanding of His goodness.

The Queen of Sheba and the Samaritan Woman

The Impact of Sincere Inquiry

After three days they found him in the temple, sitting among the teachers, listening to them and asking them questions.

Luke 2:46

My friend apologizes all the time.

She has questions. A lot of them.

She has one of the best attendance records in Bible study. She's prepared with the reading, and she always has discussion-provoking thoughts. Sometimes her questions can be uncomfortable or challenging, and that's when she apologizes. I assure her that her questions are not only welcome, but I'd miss them if she held back. I learn from them. I grow because they stretch me to consider other perspectives.

But I understand why she apologizes. She's always been an asker of hard questions, and not everyone welcomes that quality in a person. Especially a woman. Well, at least in the times in which my friend and I grew up, women's questions weren't always welcome. And sometimes they were even intentionally discouraged, treated as nuisances, or viewed as challenges to authority. I'm glad life is changing in many places on that front.

I didn't always appreciate questions in my Bible studies, not even sincere ones. Initially, I was insecure about my teaching, and questions felt threatening. I was embarrassed if I appeared unprepared or if my response was inadequate.

I once led a Bible study for a group of highly secure women who all had black belts in karate but who'd never studied the Bible. As I prepared, I'd plan for us to study and discuss . . . right up until a section that was hard to explain or where Jesus said something challenging. That was the part I'd hope to postpone. But every week, just as I was closing, one woman would scan ahead and say, "Wait a minute! What about this part? I have some questions about this next section!" My heart would sink.

But after a few weeks, God nudged me to lean into the questions instead of shrinking back. Lean in and learn. So I did. It transformed my appreciation for sincere inquiry, even when I was unprepared for difficult questions.

> **Throughout Scripture, we can see a pattern of God inviting sincere questions within the context of relationship with Him.**

God has shown me, through observation in His Word, that He welcomes hard but earnest questions. In Judges, He responded when the people "inquired of the Lord" (Judges 1:1; 20:18 and that entire chapter). King David, a man after God's own heart, inquired of the Lord often (1 Samuel 23:2, 4; 30:8) and wrote many psalms full of hard questions. Job too, as he suffered, made an impassioned appeal to God (Job 7:17–21; 13:13–28) and God answered (Job 38). The prophet Habakkuk cried out the great question his people were asking during their trial: "O Lord, how long?" (Habakkuk 1:2), and God heard.

Throughout Scripture, we can see a pattern of God inviting sincere questions within the context of relationship with Him.

Honest questions are excellent vehicles for discovery, learning, and insight. They move us to rely on God and not on our own understanding. And, if God can handle our hard questions, we can also receive them from one another. Through sincere inquiry, we both sharpen one another—"Iron sharpens iron, and one man sharpens another" (Proverbs 27:17)—and exercise patience with one another, "bearing with one another in love" (Ephesians 4:2).

Here's what I love about the Bible: every woman who asked tough questions was rewarded. From the Old Testament on through the New Testament, the askers were seen, heard, and well-received.

The Queen of Sheba traveled from far off to inquire of King Solomon. Scholars debate whether she hailed from Ethiopia or what is now modern-day Yemen. Josephus, the historian, describes her as "a woman queen of Egypt and Ethiopia."[6] Her origin may be unclear, but what is clear is that she posed difficult questions to Solomon, and he answered them all.

> Now when the queen of Sheba heard of the fame of Solomon concerning the name of the LORD, she came to test him with hard questions. She came to Jerusalem with a very great retinue, with camels bearing spices and very much gold and precious stones. And when she came to Solomon, she told him all that was on her mind. And Solomon answered all her questions; there was nothing hidden from the king that he could not explain to her. And when the queen of Sheba had seen all the wisdom of Solomon, the house that he had built, the food of his table, the seating of his officials, and the attendance of his servants, their clothing,

his cupbearers, and his burnt offerings that he offered at the house of the LORD, there was no more breath in her. (1 Kings 10:1–5)

What a wonderful representation of a king who followed the Living God! The queen of Sheba not only found their exchange breathtaking, but it also left her better off: "King Solomon gave to the queen of Sheba all that she desired, whatever she asked besides what was given her by the bounty of King Solomon" (v. 13). This spirited exchange between two powerful leaders highlights both Solomon's wisdom and generosity and the queen's curiosity, gifts, and smart choice of sincere inquiry.

Early in Israel's history, the five daughters of Zelophehad were left without parents when both died in the wilderness. By law at the time, since they were female, their father's inheritance would go to a male relative, not to them, since they had no brother. The sisters—Mahlah, Noah, Hoglah, Milcah, and Tirzah—appeared before Moses and all the leaders of Israel to make the case that they should receive what would otherwise be awarded to a male heir. Their honest question was, "Why should the name of our father be taken away from his clan because he had no son? Give to us a possession among our father's brothers" (Numbers 27:4).

Moses brought their case before God, and God agreed with the women: "The daughters of Zelophehad are right. You shall give them possession of an inheritance among their father's brothers and transfer the inheritance of their father to them" (v. 7). Moreover, He instructed Moses to change the inheritance rules for all women in the same situation. God did not hesitate to reward these five who bravely inquired of Moses and the other leaders of Israel.

Jesus also encountered a woman who asked hard questions (John 4:1–45). His disciples had gone for food, and Jesus was sitting beside Jacob's well when a Samaritan woman arrived to draw water. He asked her for a drink, and she immediately responded with a question: "How is it that you, a Jew, ask for a drink from me, a woman of Samaria?" (v. 9).

Jesus then engaged her in a lengthy exchange in which she not only asked more questions—and He asked hard questions of her in return—but He also revealed to her, a Samaritan woman, that He was the Messiah. It was such an unusual dialogue that the disciples marveled at it.

Some read her questions as an attempt to divert Jesus from His line of inquiry. But it's just as likely this was simply a bright, thoughtful woman, often overlooked because of her situation, who seized an opportunity because Jesus made it safe to do so. She was enthralled by Jesus and His answers. She was inspired to return to her town and tell everyone she knew. And as a result, many were convinced that Jesus was the Messiah.

The outcome of the queen of Sheba's sincere inquiry was to enrich both nations and spread Solomon's fame even further. The end of the five sisters' hard question was to change the inheritance laws for other women. The Samaritan woman's graceful influence was not only to spread news of Jesus to her people but also to provide the rest of us with breathtaking insights from Jesus through their conversation. Her courageous inquiries benefit us all.

People who ask hard questions in God's kingdom often receive not only answers but blessings that leave them breathless in wonder and gratitude. When Israel inquired of God, God led them. When Israel's kings inquired of God, God blessed them. When Job inquired of God, God answered him and restored his fortunes (including blessing him with ten more children: seven sons, and three daughters, Jemimah, Keziah, and Keren-happuch).

All these people chose to ask hard but authentic questions, questions without guile or challenge to God's authority. They seem driven by genuine curiosity and eagerness to understand, gain direction, or call for just treatment. God is clearly able to sort out honest inquirers from those looking to rebel.

Are you always bursting with hard questions? Take heart. Though others may sigh or grow weary, though some may even have tried to silence your voice, God receives you, and His response just might take your breath away.

BIBLE

People asked Jesus questions all the time, but they didn't all have curious hearts. Sometimes, as in Matthew 22:15–22, they were testing Him. What is the difference between inquiring sincerely, like the Samaritan woman, versus testing God with questions, like the Pharisees?

Bible Extra

Another stark example of contrasting questions occurs when both Zechariah and Mary were visited by the angel Gabriel, who announced the coming births of John the Baptist and Jesus.

Zechariah responded, "How shall I know this? For I am an old man, and my wife is advanced in years" (Luke 1:18). Gabriel told him his unbelief would result in his being unable to speak until John's birth. Zechariah's question was a challenge emerging from an incredulous heart.

Mary inquired too upon hearing Gabriel's announcement, but she asked, "How will this be, since I am a virgin?" (v. 34). She believed Gabriel but was curious (understandably) about how the conception would occur. Gabriel then simply provided her information (vv. 35–38).

Jesus asked questions of the rabbis as a young man, and He continued to use questions with His disciples, the crowds, and the Pharisees. Sincere inquiry is different than challenging authority or expressing unbelief and is clearly welcomed by God.

BATTLE

The battle here is between remaining silent or sincerely inquiring. It's reasonable to believe there were women in Bible times who let their hard questions go unasked, out of either fear or repression. They remained hidden in the crowds. But life and faith are loaded with hard questions. Asking them from genuine hearts with respect for God could lead us to receive exactly the answers or the outcomes we seek.

Bottom Line

People who make sincere inquiries of God often
receive not only answers but also blessings
that leave them breathless with wonder.

The Wise Woman of Abel, and Euodia and Syntyche

The Impact of Peacemaking

*Blessed are the peacemakers, for they
shall be called sons of God.*

Matthew 5:9

We've all experienced conflict—a bickering couple, a tense staff huddle, clashing views in a church meeting. But ongoing or unresolved conflict can wear us out.

It is this strength-sapping aspect of division, argument, and estrangement that should especially concern us. Jesus followers need every ounce of strength for life and work in Christ.

It should also concern us that Jesus emphasized the unity of believers when He prayed, "I do not ask for these only, but also for those who will believe in me through their word, that they may all be one, just as you, Father, are in me, and I in you, that they also may be in us, so that the world may believe that you have sent me"(John 17:20–21). Our unity inspires belief that Jesus was indeed sent by God.

And yet we argue. And yet we divide. And yet we live with ongoing, unresolved conflict.

God has called us to be peacemakers. Conflict is the default mode of our sin nature. We must choose to do the work that leads to peace.

This is a complex undertaking, requiring discernment. For just as all unity isn't godly, neither is all peace. The peace created through compromise or watering down the truth is no peace. Some division is a result of people's separating from heresy or from ungodly practices. Some arguments result from holding others accountable for their sin. Resistance to repentance can create ongoing conflict or even estrangement.

Yes, there are valid, biblical reasons for conflict; nevertheless, too much disagreement stems from our own sin and self-centeredness. It can be resolved if we access the peacemaking power of Christ within and between us. Too often, though, we throw up our hands and stand by, hoping someone else will do the hard work.

Paul, in his letter to the Philippians, mentioned a conflict between two women that was hurting the church in Philippi. The church there had begun with a group of women Paul and his team had visited: "On the Sabbath day we went outside the gate to the riverside, where we supposed there was a place of prayer, and we sat down and spoke to the women who had come together" (Acts 16:13).

The apostle encountered women who "had come together" for prayer. It is a powerful act when people come together for that reason. We know then that God is in our midst (Matthew 18:20). So of course our enemy will seek to thwart all such efforts. This group became the foundation of the Philippian church. Later on, however, Satan found a foothold in a disagreement between two of the women, Euodia and Syntyche.

Paul used emphatic language, pleading with the two to resolve their differences: "I entreat Euodia and I entreat Syntyche to agree in the Lord. Yes, I ask you also, true companion, help these women, who have labored side by side with me in the gospel together with Clement and the rest of my fellow workers, whose names are in the book of life" (Philippians 4:2–3).

His entreaty demonstrates the importance of resolving conflict between believers. Paul laid the responsibility for that not only on the women involved but also on others who might support them in working through their difference. He called on the peacemakers because these two had, for this moment, turned their backs on this aspect of their discipleship, and it was hurting the church.

I understand this situation. I've had times when a particular disagreement with another believer loomed larger in my perspective than the greater calling of the gospel. It's easy to get caught up, dig in, and forget what matters. It's easier to separate than to swallow pride and commit to creating peace. Two keys for motivating me to come to the table when disagreements arise are (a) trusting Jesus's teaching on the importance of maintaining unity, and (b) remembering that our enemy wants to keep us divided because it serves his purposes.

The immediate effect of the two women's conflict was, clearly, that it disrupted the work of the church in Philippi enough to distress Paul in prison. The widespread influence of church conflict is all around us.

The result of choosing not to make peace is widespread disillusionment with the church, confusion, and a dilution of the message of the gospel. Generations may be damaged, especially when impressionable children or teens witness division and church conflict that goes unresolved. Disagreement can disrupt years of godly parenting and send children out the church doors for decades.

On this side of glory, no church will be free of conflict, but the world doesn't need a church free of conflict. The world needs a church unafraid of conflict, filled with people who choose to do the hard work of resolving it, empowered by the Holy Spirit.

There was an Old Testament woman, the wise woman of Abel, who chose to be instrumental in peacemaking and saved her entire city from destruction. In the wake of Absalom's attempted coup (2 Samuel 15–19), the kingdom of Israel was regrouping. Samuel then penned some frank words about a man named Sheba: "Now there happened to be there a worthless man, whose name was Sheba" (2 Samuel 20:1). We've all probably known someone like Sheba who doesn't think and consequently puts others in danger.

Sheba rebelled against King David's leadership. The men of Israel followed him, withdrawing their loyalty from the king. The people of Judah, however, remained faithful to David. Seeing that Sheba's rebellion would harm the kingdom even more than Absalom's betrayal, David wisely sent the soldiers of Judah along with his mighty men, led by Joab, in pursuit of Sheba.

The rebel leader had holed up in a city called Abel of Beth-maacah. Joab and his troops surrounded the city, building a siege ramp and battering the walls. Joab and his army would have fought their way in, certainly destroying many in their path and leaving the city vulnerable to attack from others, if it weren't for one brave, wise, peacemaking woman. "Then a wise woman called from the city, 'Listen! Listen! Tell Joab, "Come here, that I may speak to you."'" (v. 16).

When Joab came near, she called down, "They used to say in former times, 'Let them but ask counsel at Abel,' and so they settled a matter. I am one of those who are peaceable and faithful in Israel. You seek to destroy a city that is a mother in Israel. Why will you swallow up the heritage of the Lord?" (vv. 18–19).

Joab let this woman know they were only after Sheba. If they could have him, they would spare the city.

"And the woman said to Joab, 'Behold, his head shall be

thrown to you over the wall.' Then the woman went to all the people in her wisdom. And they cut off the head of Sheba the son of Bichri and threw it out to Joab. So he blew the trumpet, and they dispersed from the city, every man to his home. And Joab returned to Jerusalem to the king" (vv. 21–22). Not a pretty story, but then, the process of resolving conflict seldom is. Peace*making* is not for the faint of heart.

My daughter loved tuna casserole when she was small, until one day she watched me make it. Once she realized what went into it, the dish lost its appeal. It can be like that with peacemaking. We all love and appreciate the outcome of peace, but we struggle to watch as it's being created.

The wise woman of Abel drew on years of practiced discernment and conflict resolution to muster the courage to confront Joab. She chose not to hide from conflict but to engage with tools that create peace. The end of her actions was the deliverance of that city and generations of citizens as well as the restoration of Israel as one under King David.

As for Euodia and Syntyche, we don't learn the outcome of their conflict. Perhaps God allowed it to remain a mystery so we'd carefully reflect on any disunity in our lives. Most translations also leave us to wonder who the "true companion" is that Paul asked to mediate. Rev. Eugene Peterson translated it in *The Message* as the proper name Syzygus, meaning "one who works well in a yoke." The implication is that the women weren't working well together, pulling against their yoke. They would benefit from a peacemaker experienced at teaming with others.

Whoever the mystery person was, Paul trusted him or her to intervene and do the hard work leading to peace (although I'm sure that, unlike Sheba, no one lost their head).

What holds you back from waging peace? What restrains you from settling your conflicts and then using those skills to assist others? Blessed indeed are the peacemakers.

Where are you, peacemakers? Can you come out from the shadows now to help the church in our generation forge the peace for which Jesus prayed? The lasting impact will be eternal.

> Where are you, peacemakers? Can you come out from the shadows now to help the church in our generation forge the peace for which Jesus prayed?

BIBLE

Read Ephesians 4:1–6 and 2 Corinthians 5:18–21. Within the church, we're called to maintain our unity. At other times, we're exhorted to engage in the ministry of reconciliation, which implies helping unbelievers be reconciled with Jesus. What is it about seeing those of us within the church live at peace with one another that might attract others to Christ?

Was Solomon possibly considering the story of the wise woman of Abel when he wrote, "Wisdom is better than weapons of war, but one sinner destroys much good" (Ecclesiastes 9:18)? What is your reaction to that verse?

Bible Extra

Second Samuel 14 records another wise woman, this one from Tekoa, hired by Joab to intervene with King David about his son Absalom. Her actions helped bring peace to the kingdom and peace between father and son, at least for a time.

BATTLE

Even after we've come to Christ, there's a part of us that just wants what it wants. As His Holy Spirit does the work of making us more like Him, that part has less sway over our actions, but we're wise to be aware of it. When we argue, we're well served if someone who loves each party comes alongside and assists with resolution. Peacemakers are discerning, wise, self-aware, grounded in God's Word, and attuned to the Holy Spirit. They must also be brave. As hard as it is, the graceful influence of peacemaking is a stronger witness for Christ.

Bottom Line

The world doesn't need a church free of conflict; the world needs a church unafraid of conflict because of the power of the Holy Spirit.

22

Dinah, Tamar, and Bathsheba

The Impact of Persevering through Trial

This I call to mind, and therefore I have hope: The steadfast love of the LORD never ceases; his mercies never come to an end.

Lamentations 3:21–22

Sexual assault. Child abuse. Domestic violence. Human trafficking. The death or murder of a child. Kidnapping. Imprisonment. Genocide. War.

Women around the world suffer unimaginable traumas every day. The list of ways a woman can be victimized in a fallen world astounds. Too often, we allow silence in our Christian circles around these topics because simply recounting them creates such discomfort. They are the Bible stories seldom told. But it's important that we tell them so other victims know God is present with them even through the worst.

God doesn't endorse the victimization of women. He also doesn't let Scripture remain silent about the reality of it. Crimes are described. Aggressors are named. The biblical record is clear that God witnessed what happened, even behind closed doors. He will deliver justice in due time.

But what of the women? What of their lives after their abuse?

Women in ancient cultures frequently had less freedom than we do, but there is a decision we can make after the worst has happened. It's an attitude within our own minds, hearts, and souls. It is so private, it can be overlooked or underestimated. This shift in thinking may be nothing more than a flicker of resolve, but it can make all the difference. That is the choice to persevere through trial.

Even now, we cannot choose everything that happens to us, but we can determine our internal response. We can remember that others don't have the final word on our lives—God does. We can persevere.

Helen Roseveare is one who persevered through trial. Helen was a medical missionary from England who served in Africa for decades starting in 1953. She endured many challenges, frustrations, and discomforts daily as part of her work serving the people's medical and spiritual needs. But in 1964, civil war broke out in the Congo. Helen was among other Protestant missionaries taken captive, beaten, imprisoned for months, and brutally raped. Years later, having persevered through her terrible trial, Roseveare said, "Through the brutal heartbreaking experience of rape, God met with me—with outstretched arms of love."[7]

Dr. Roseveare survived her experience and went on to write books, speaking around the world about the love and power of Jesus Christ. God provided healing beyond trauma and she remained engaged with life until her death at age ninety-one.

Dinah, Tamar, and Bathsheba are biblical women who also experienced sexual victimization. For two of them, we learn little more beyond that story.

Dinah was the only sister of Jacob's twelve sons. One day she went out "to see the women of the land" (Genesis 34:1). Sadly, "when Shechem the son of Hamor the Hivite, the prince of the land, saw her, he seized her and lay with her and humiliated her" (v. 2). That description is disturbing in its stark summation of the moment that stole a young woman's entire future.

Except for mentions of her name in lists of Jacob's children, this is all we hear of Dinah. She's given no voice in this biblical narrative; we only know the response of the men around her.

Shechem, through Hamor, requested to marry her. Jacob heard what happened but waited for her brothers to return from work. The outraged brothers deceived Hamor, agreeing to the union only on condition that the men of their city be circumcised. When the men were recovering, Simeon and Levi slaughtered them.

No one was right. Not the man who assaulted Dinah nor his father. Not Jacob in his silence. Not her brothers' violence. Tragically, Dinah's narrative ends here.

King David's daughter Tamar was victimized by her half brother, Amnon. Amnon lusted after Tamar (2 Samuel 13:1–33), so his scheming friend, Jonadab, convinced him to fake an illness and beg the king to send Tamar to prepare food for him. David complied, and Tamar unwittingly went to comfort Amnon.

Amnon sent everyone else out and forced himself on Tamar despite her resistance and pleas for him to stop. Once he'd raped her, Amnon hated her as much as he'd desired her and put her out of his residence, utterly bereft and humiliated. Tamar wailed loudly, tearing her robe in despair. "And her brother Absalom said to her, 'Has Amnon your brother been with you? Now hold your peace, my sister. He is your brother; do not take this to heart.' So Tamar lived, a desolate woman, in her brother Absalom's house. When King David heard of all these things, he was very angry" (2 Samuel 13:20–21).

David took no action against Amnon for his crime. Absalom eventually arranged for his half brother's murder. Absalom's words to Tamar certainly sound dismissive, but perhaps he was trying to mask his own devastation or comfort her in his own way. We don't know. Absalom provided her a home and eventually named his daughter Tamar, possibly in his sister's honor. But his sister remained desolate.

Again what stands out is the violence and silence of the men as well as the desolation of the woman and her absence in the story from there on.

Bathsheba is well known. We encounter her during King David's infamous moral lapse (2 Samuel 11). He slept with Bathsheba, the wife of one of his "mighty men," Uriah. Then, when she became pregnant with his child, David arranged Uriah's death.

While this is often listed as David's adultery, what we read from the text indicates Bathsheba may have had little voice in the union. Back then, David, being male, a warrior, and king, would have had all the power in the relationship. David wasn't where he was supposed to be (2 Samuel 11:1), and Bathsheba was. Verse 4 uses strong words to say, "So David sent messengers and took her, and she came to him, and he lay with her." We just can't know how much consent Bathsheba could give.

On hearing of Uriah's death, Bathsheba lamented him. Then when she had finished mourning, David took her to his home, married her, and she bore their son. But Bathsheba's story doesn't end there.

God confronted David through the prophet Nathan and condemned his sin. David's offence was great, and as a leader, he reaped its consequences, which also inevitably affected the people around him. The sword would never depart from David's house. Because he took Uriah's wife, David's wives would in turn be similarly taken. And the child born to David and Bathsheba would die.

Despite these great trials and losses, Bathsheba persevered and appears to have remained engaged with life. "David comforted his wife, Bathsheba, and went in to her and lay with her, and she bore a son, and he called his name Solomon. And the LORD loved him and sent a message by Nathan the prophet. So he called his name Jedidiah, because of the LORD" (2 Samuel 12:24–25). Jedidiah means "beloved of the Lord." Bathsheba received this word that God looked with favor on her son, Solomon. Perhaps it was during this time that she decided to persevere despite her trials.

Bathsheba's graceful influence surfaces toward the end of David's life when he was so old and frail, Abishag the Shunammite was assigned to keep him warm (1 Kings 1:1–4). David's officials knew God had appointed Solomon to be his successor (1 Chronicles 28:5). However, that succession was challenged when Adonijah, David's fourth son, declared himself heir to the throne. Nathan the prophet came to Bathsheba and said, "Let me give you advice, that you may save your own life and the life of your son Solomon" (1 Kings 1:12). Heeding Nathan's counsel, Bathsheba intervened with David. She reminded him of his promise and secured Solomon's reign.

> **There is hope in choosing to engage with life for another day, and then another.**

Bathsheba's perseverance through trial and advocacy for her son's survival resulted in preserving the appointment of Israel's wisest king. She is also included in the messianic line (Matthew 1:6).

Other than mentioning Tamar's desolation, Scripture is silent on her and Dinah following their assaults. Did they find peace for themselves within their brothers' households? Or did they live as shadows? We just don't know. However, we do see that Bathsheba remained engaged with life. While certainly not finding any fault with the first two women, we can find hope in the one who clearly persevered.

There is strength in persevering through trial. There is hope in choosing to engage with life for another day, and then another. We sometimes make this choice incrementally from beneath the rubble, or from inside the bandages, or while healing, or while battling depression. But with God and the help of others, we can rise from the ashes of unimaginable fires. By the grace of God, we can persevere through overwhelming trials and live to write new chapters in our stories.

BIBLE

It can be distressing to read the stories of these women and all they endured. Many women appreciate the counterbalance account of Jael, who was not a victim but a victor—a defender of women. Christians aren't encouraged to commit violence or disregard the value of a human soul, but when others resort to evil, we do defend the defenseless. Jael chose to defend Israel (Judges 4:17–24), and Deborah celebrated her (5:24–31). Her bravery likely prevented the assault of many Israelite women as Deborah declared in her song. Imagining Sisera's mother wondering why he took so long to return, Deborah sang. "Have they not found and divided the spoil?—A womb or two for every man" (v. 30). Jael prevented a common horror of war for a generation of Israelite women.

Bible Extra

"Blessed is the man who remains steadfast under trial, for when he has stood the test he will receive the crown of life, which God has promised to those who love him" (James 1:12). We may suffer many types of trials in this life, including sexual trauma, but God can help us persevere through it all.

BATTLE

To say it isn't easy to choose to persevere in the face of the unthinkable is a vast understatement. Women who face unimaginable horrors are often traumatized and changed in ways others cannot fathom. And yet, many choose to look to God to help them endure.

By God's grace, many receive the support, professional assistance, and practical aid their hearts require to persevere. As a church, we can do better at acknowledging their struggle. We can make it safer for women (and men) to share their stories—to say aloud what happened and testify to God's deliverance, not only from the disaster but from the temptation to surrender to the death of their body, mind, or soul. The church needs the voices of these survivors because every generation must remember again the words of Romans 12:21: "Do not be overcome by evil, but overcome evil with good."

Bottom Line

With God and the help of others, we
can persevere through trial, rising from
the ashes of unimaginable fires.

Foolish Virgins and Wise Virgins

The Impact of Preparation

Two women will be grinding at the mill; one will be taken and one left. Therefore, stay awake, for you do not know on what day your Lord is coming.

Matthew 24:41–42

In the days leading up to major hurricanes, leaders plead with those in the direct path of the storm to prepare.

They issue ever more urgent warnings. Officials at every level of government post lists of necessary supplies, instructions for securing homes, and directions to designated storm shelters. Then, as the storm becomes a certainty, they take to the airwaves and send first responders to knock on doors, aiming to persuade those who will most likely need assistance or be stranded to evacuate and wait out the storm. Some people listen.

Then, there are the others.

In the days leading up to Hurricane Sandy in 2012, one governor became extremely frustrated with the hundreds of people ignoring his warnings to prepare. While thousands heeded him, preparing their homes and then volunteering to help neighbors or fill sandbags for the town, many scoffed and mocked those who prepared.

They'd weathered plenty of storms with no major issues.

The meteorologists just liked making a big deal out of a little wind. It would come to nothing, and they'd be the ones who looked smart.

Everyone should just calm down. Those running around preparing were just overreacting to a little wind and rain. How bad could it be?

Hurricane Sandy became a superstorm and was one of the deadliest and most destructive hurricanes of that year. In eight countries, from the Caribbean to the United States to Canada, the storm took 233 lives and caused almost $70 billion in damage.[8] Preparedness often made the difference between life and death.

Preparedness also makes that difference with two groups of women Jesus described in His parable of the ten virgins. He told this parable in the context of talking about His second coming. He warned in Matthew 24 that no one knows the day or time, so we must always be ready. Watch and wait, expectant and prepared. Then in chapter 25 He told this story:

> The kingdom of heaven will be like ten virgins who took their lamps and went to meet the bridegroom. Five of them were foolish, and five were wise. For when the foolish took their lamps, they took no oil with them, but the wise took flasks of oil with their lamps. (vv. 1–4)

Can't you just imagine the mothers in the crowd exchanging glances and knowing nods as He described the difference in attitude between these two groups of young women? Five of the girls prepared. Five did not. Oh yes, the mothers had seen that happen. They knew girls like that.

> As the bridegroom was delayed, they all became
> drowsy and slept. (v. 5)

Those hearing the story would have nodded again. After an Israelite couple was betrothed in those times, the groom went off to prepare a place for his bride. Within the year, he was expected to return to have the wedding, but no one knew exactly when because he would come only upon completing his preparation.

During this time, the bride prepared her wedding garments, lamps, and so on with the help of other unmarried women her age. Immediately after the betrothal, of course, there would be a flurry of activity, but as the weeks and sometimes months went on, languor may have set in for some—a falling off from expectancy and quite possibly some procrastination.

Our traditions may vary, but one thing remains consistent: some bridesmaids spearhead all the preparation while other bridesmaids show up at the last minute expecting the same reception and benefits.

Jesus continued:

> At midnight there was a cry, "Here is the bride-
> groom! Come out to meet him." Then all those
> virgins rose and trimmed their lamps. And the
> foolish said to the wise, "Give us some of your
> oil, for our lamps are going out." But the wise
> answered, saying, "Since there will not be enough
> for us and for you, go rather to the dealers and
> buy for yourselves." (vv. 6–9)

Unless you've been the mother of a bride or groom, that last verse might sound selfish of the wise women, but the prepared virgins understood something vital about this event: it was not about them.

The wedding was about the bride and groom. These virgins understood that their role was to be ready to contribute to the celebration. They weren't going to hold things up or create a distraction because others had failed to prepare.

The point of this parable is, of course, to prepare for the coming Christ. As much as we may love and feel compassion for those who don't obtain oil for their lamps by accepting Jesus before He comes, we cannot lend them our salvation. They cannot light their lamps on oil from our redemption. They need to accept Jesus now and be ready.

Jesus explained why.

> While they were going to buy, the bridegroom came, and those who were ready went in with him to the marriage feast, and the door was shut. Afterward the other virgins came also, saying, "Lord, lord, open to us." But he answered, "Truly, I say to you, I do not know you." Watch therefore, for you know neither the day nor the hour. (vv. 10–13)

It's one thing to appreciate variations in personality type and indulge people's idiosyncrasies in preparing either far in advance or at the last minute. We can and do bear with one another in love, and God does too.

But there are situations—life-threatening hurricanes; the looming threat of an eternity separated from God—that create realities no one should ignore.

To choose to prepare for the day of Jesus's coming is to choose eternal life. To choose to remain unprepared is to risk eternity shut out from all that is beautiful, good, loving, holy, just, and true. That is a seriously lasting impact.

Peter explains that Jesus's return isn't long in coming because God has forgotten or has changed His mind (2 Peter 3:9–10). Instead, He is giving opportunity for as many as possible to enter relationship with Jesus. Like the long-awaited bridegroom in the parable, however, Jesus will one day appear suddenly, and every event will commence quickly—just as He has promised.

The decision to prepare for Jesus's coming may be the simplest to explain, but it is the most important one to make.

God prepares. He prepared good works beforehand for us (Ephesians 2:10). He is preparing a place for us with Him (John 14:2–3). He has prepared a city for people of faith (Hebrews 11:16). He has prepared things we can't even imagine right now (1 Corinthians 2:9).

In the days of Noah, as that man of faith took decades to build the ark, God gave people time to prepare for the coming flood. Only Noah and his family listened, and so only they were saved through the waters. Likewise, now He has given all of us time to prepare for the coming judgment. It will come.

> **The decision to prepare for Jesus's coming may be the simplest to explain, but it is the most important one to make.**

Who will be prepared by entering a saving relationship with Jesus Christ? How can we support people now to be those who are prepared with oil for their lamps when the Bridegroom returns?

BIBLE

Read Matthew 25:36–46. How do we "keep watch" as Jesus instructed? How do we remain awake and ready for His return? What are signs that we're "falling asleep"?

It's significant that the Bible promises in Hebrews 4 that we will one day enter God's rest. But we are not living in that day. We're living in times when we must remain alert. God's Word warns, "So then let us not sleep, as others do, but let us keep awake and be sober" (1 Thessalonians 5:6). That doesn't mean we should never physically sleep but that there is so much at stake regarding people's souls, we can't be drowsy in matters of faith. We must keep our minds available to reason and to make sound decisions.

Bible Extra

Romans 10:9 says, "If you confess with your mouth that Jesus is Lord and believe in your heart that God raised him from the dead, you will be saved." If you have not prepared for His coming by confessing Jesus with your mouth and believing in your heart that God raised Him from the dead, Jesus invites you to do this right now.

BATTLE

We truly are in a battle for souls. Many modern people struggle to prepare dinner, never mind preparing for eternity. This matter can fall off people's radar or never even appear as a blip on their screen unless we who know Christ raise the subject and point the way.

Believers must always remain alert. Alert for opportunities to discuss spiritual topics. Alert for the signs Jesus taught that would point the way to His return. Alert to moments of readiness in those who have yet to enter a relationship with Jesus.

We must appreciate the importance of this decision to prepare for eternity for those who don't yet understand its priority. We battle not only human nature and sin but also an enemy who seeks to keep us all distracted. What do we need to do to remain watchful and awake to prepare for His return?

There is no greater eternal influence than to lead someone to prepare wisely to greet Him.

Bottom Line

He has given us all time to prepare for His return.

Medium of En-dor and Lydia

The Impact of Godly Work

She perceives that her merchandise is profitable.
Her lamp does not go out at night.

Proverbs 31:18

In ancient times, women worked hard at numerous professions, even sometimes as owners or business managers.

It's often said that prostitution is the world's oldest profession. Prostitution draws attention, but there were other opportunities mentioned in the Bible for women. Opportunities we simply skim over because they are less sensationalized.

Home and work weren't as delineated then as they are in modern times since much work was a family affair. Women were shepherdesses, seamstresses, shopkeepers, cooks, farmers, and midwives. Some women served as judges or prophetesses. Everyone labored, even young people. Everyone contributed on some level, and some women received remuneration for their work.

That isn't to say there was equality in ancient societies, but managing households required a range of skills on everyone's part—everything from teaching children, to bartering at the market, to keeping household records, to helping with the family trade. From household to household, what a wife or daughter was able to do varied. A widow depended on sons or other male relatives to treat her fairly, but it would help if she had means for contributing to the household.

As with every situation facing women and men, women could choose to either honor God with their work or not. The witch or medium of En-dor chose not to honor God, at least in the one instance recorded in Scripture. We don't know if she was an Israelite or simply living in Israel, but she clearly knew the law prohibiting mediums and necromancers.

Old Testament Scripture was clear that God disapproves of consulting mediums or engaging in divination or witchcraft. "Do not turn to mediums or necromancers; do not seek them out, and so make yourselves unclean by them: I am the LORD your God" (Leviticus 19:31), and "If a person turns to mediums and necromancers, whoring after them, I will set my face against that person and will cut him off from among his people" (20:6).

Isaiah suggests that these commands exist because we are to consult the Living God rather than consult with the dead. "When they say to you, 'Inquire of the mediums and the necromancers who chirp and mutter,' should not a people inquire of their God? Should they inquire of the dead on behalf of the living?" (Isaiah 8:19).

The witch or medium of En-dor chose a profession that put her in conflict with the law of Moses and the God of Israel. En-dor was in the land assigned to the tribe of Manasseh, one of Joseph's sons. Then, as now, there were markets for what was forbidden, and this woman allowed herself to be persuaded to operate in that realm. She may have previously been abiding by the laws and experienced a lapse under Saul's persuasion—a lesson for us all about momentary compromise.

All the land mourned the prophet Samuel, none more than

Saul (1 Samuel 28). He faced a battle with the Philistines and had inquired of God by the acceptable means but received no answer. Of course, he shouldn't have expected one as he had already lost God's backing because of his previous sins (13:8–14).

But now, Saul had a problem. He had put the mediums and necromancers out of the land (28:9). As we know, Saul could make a public show of allegiance to God but struggled with private obedience. Now, as in the past, Saul grew impatient, and so he set out in disguise (v. 8) to consult this medium living in En-dor.

Initially, the medium expressed suspicion because she knew the king had outlawed her practice, but she did eventually cooperate and called up the spirit of Samuel. Much to her surprise, Samuel appeared. With that, the woman realized the stranger with whom she was doing business was King Saul (v. 12).

Samuel delivered a message to Saul, beginning with a stern reminder that Saul had lost God's favor and support. Samuel told Saul that on the next day, God would deliver Israel to the Philistines and Saul and his sons to death (v. 19). Saul, overcome by fear and hunger, fell prostrate, but the medium, along with Saul's men, encouraged him to rise and eat (vv. 20–25).

There's clearly great disobedience and sadness in the story. What makes it sadder is that this woman appears to have been bright and ready to exercise compassion. Just as Saul's story could have been one of faith, her story might have been one too, had she chosen obedience.

Both the medium and Saul were living and working in the land of the God of Israel. They both acknowledged the spiritual realm. But each disobeyed. Each made something more important than God. Self? Financial gain? Power? People's opinions? We don't know their hearts, but we see their choices. Rather than apply her intelligence, compassion, and business mind to work that was acceptable to God, the medium exercised a forbidden practice that perpetuated sin in Israel. Her immediate influence was to provide Israel's king with the means to disobey God.

In contrast, Lydia was a businesswoman from Thyatira living in Philippi during the time of the New Testament. She was "a seller of purple goods" (Acts 16:14). Lydia's hometown was a center of trade, particularly of indigo, a dye made from small Mediterranean mollusks. So Lydia would have been both a tradeswoman and a keeper of the art of cloth dyeing. Her richly colored fabric was affordable only to the wealthy and families of the royals. There is some archaeological evidence of a dyer's guild in Philippi, which may explain why Lydia was there from Thyatira. Lacking details, we can only speculate.

We have just a brief passage about Lydia:

> On the Sabbath day we went outside the gate to the riverside, where we supposed there was a place of prayer, and we sat down and spoke to the women who had come together. One who heard us was a woman named Lydia, from the city of Thyatira, a seller of purple goods, who was a worshiper of God. The Lord opened her heart to pay attention to what was said by Paul. And after she was baptized, and her household as well, she urged us, saying, "If you have judged me to be faithful to the Lord, come to my house and stay." And she prevailed upon us. (Acts 16:13–15)

Here's what we know: Lydia was a faithful God-worshiper. Men weren't gathered for prayer on the Sabbath, but Lydia and other women were. Paul and his company were not put off by their gender but shared the gospel with these women. God opened Lydia's heart to the truth of Jesus, and she was baptized—not just alone but with her entire household. This speaks well to her graceful influence over those who lived with her and served in her residence.

Immediately her faith translated into action. She opened her home to Paul and the missionary team with him. As a businesswoman, she likely looked at life in practical terms and realized the apostle would need a base of operation, food, and shelter. Lydia is considered the first convert in Europe, and this was likely one of the first places of home worship.

Out of the means and profits of her business, Lydia offered hospitality to those who brought to her the good news of salvation in Jesus. Much as the women following Jesus supported Him out of their means, Lydia's generosity was a support to this new chapter of the gospel. She immediately chose to honor God with her profits and professional skills in the birthplace of the church in Philippi.

BIBLE

It's interesting that the conversion of Lydia was one of three significant events in Philippi, all recorded in Acts 16 and all affecting working people. Besides bringing Lydia to faith, Paul and Silas cast demons out of a slave girl, angering those who profited from her skills. Then, in the aftermath of the earthquake that followed the two men's arrest, their jailer was converted. Fearing all his prisoners had escaped, he was about to take his own life when Paul assured him everyone was still there. The jailer had seen enough. He and his household were baptized.

Whether drawing on family resources or their personal earnings, women chose to generously support Jesus's ministry out of their own means (Luke 8:1–3). Paul commends Phoebe to the Romans and describes her as a patron of his and many others (Romans 16:2). And the woman described in Proverbs 31 used both her artisanship and her business acumen to serve God and care for her household.

Bible Extra

The ministry of the apostles disrupted and transformed the social and economic order with the news of the gospel. We sometimes lose sight of this in our times. Yet it remains true that changed lives and corresponding action are clear evidence of the foundational change Jesus brings to our lives, families, and livelihoods.

What does Colossians 3:23–24 contribute to your thinking about the relationship of faith to your business or work endeavors?

BATTLE

In many ways, life and work were more integrated in biblical times than today. While things are trending back in that direction, we still face a battle around compartmentalizing our work, as if generating an income is somehow separate from our relationship with Jesus.

I believe that was Peter's outlook when Jesus told him to push out again after a long night of fishing with no result (Luke 5:1–11). The size of the catch impressed on Peter that Jesus knew Peter's business even better than Peter did. He knows ours better than we do too.

Jesus changes everything. It can be disruptive to invite Him into our work and professional life, but that disruption can lead to blessing beyond our imagination.

Bottom Line

Women in biblical times could choose to either
honor God with their work or defy Him. So can we.

25

Naomi and the Widow's Mite

The Impact of Giving

He who supplies seed to the sower and bread for food
will supply and multiply your seed for sowing and
increase the harvest of your righteousness. You will
be enriched in every way to be generous in every way,
which through us will produce thanksgiving to God.

2 Corinthians 9:10–11

In the economics of biblical truth, even the poor can live in an abundance of spirit, and the rich can find themselves soul poor.

My husband and I have always had to budget carefully. We've seen times when that budget didn't stretch quite far enough. Sometimes God supplied our financial need through unexpected resources. Other times, He supplied wisdom so we could make better choices. And then there were times He supplied faith that even though our finances were falling short, His love and grace never do. I have spent a lifetime wrestling with how to live generously and trust in the abundance God provides.

Several years ago I determined, after much prayer, that it would cost me nothing and gain me great peace of mind to live believing I have enough. I stopped looking at my lack more than I looked at my blessings. I trusted what the psalmist wrote in Psalm 84:11: "No good thing does he withhold from those who walk uprightly." And as I walked in this way, I began to experience the joy of a generous spirit even when finances were tight.

Peter assured us that we have everything we need for life and godliness in Jesus Christ (2 Peter 1:3). We can choose to live generously, giving freely of our time, our resources, and our hearts because God supplies our every need in Jesus (Philippians 4:19). Or we can live grasping and clinging, as if we fear God may withhold something good from us.

Naomi and her husband left the land of the Israelites to seek what they needed in the land of the Moabites. They lived in the days when the judges ruled and a famine was upon Israel. While in Moab, Naomi's husband and sons died, leaving her bitter and bereft.

Naomi returned to Israel, and her daughter-in-law Ruth chose to follow Naomi and her God (Ruth 1:16), despite their trying circumstances. This should have brought Naomi comfort. She could have looked on the blessing of this young woman as a kindness from God.

Instead, Naomi wrapped her bitterness and grief around herself like a shroud.

> So the two of them went on until they came to Bethlehem. And when they came to Bethlehem, the whole town was stirred because of them. And the women said, "Is this Naomi?" She said to them, "Do not call me Naomi; call me Mara, for the Almighty has dealt very bitterly with me. I went away full, and the LORD has brought me back empty. Why call me Naomi, when the LORD has testified

against me and the Almighty has brought calamity
upon me?" (Ruth 1:19–21)

Naomi means "pleasant." Mara means "bitter."

Naomi left no question as to her choice of spirit. Furthermore, she laid all the blame for her troubles on God. Naomi discounted the blessing of the faithful daughter-in-law beside her and embraced self-pity. She clung to her emptiness and threw it back at God as if He was withholding from her while blessing everyone else.

Ruth had come to this land as empty as Naomi, maybe more so. Ruth was also widowed. She'd left her homeland and all that was familiar to her. And she'd remained devoted to a mother-in-law who clutched her own empty pockets like they were hard evidence against the Almighty.

But rather than follow this path of living in her wounds, Ruth embraced the God of Israel and the ways of her adopted people. She worked hard and provided for her mother-in-law. Her generous spirit became known among the people.

When she encountered Boaz, who would become her husband, he said to Ruth,

> All that you have done for your mother-in-law
> since the death of your husband has been fully told
> to me, and how you left your father and mother
> and your native land and came to a people that
> you did not know before. The LORD repay you for
> what you have done, and a full reward be given you
> by the LORD, the God of Israel, under whose wings
> you have come to take refuge! (Ruth 2:11–12)

This passage contains a powerful key to understanding abundance and giving. Ruth and Naomi both returned empty, but Ruth took refuge under God's wings. Naomi withheld her gratitude and her blessing toward God and sought refuge in bitterness.

Even still, God blessed Naomi through Ruth. Naomi gleaned healing from the hard work, faithfulness, and generosity of Ruth. Boaz married Ruth, becoming her kinsman-redeemer, and God blessed Naomi with a grandson, Obed (which means "servant or worshiper of God").

The women of the village looked to redirect Naomi's heart, telling her, "Blessed be the Lord, who has not left you this day without a redeemer, and may his name be renowned in Israel! He shall be to you a restorer of life and a nourisher of your old age, for your daughter-in-law who loves you, who is more to you than seven sons, has given birth to him" (Ruth 4:14–15).

The women referred to Obed as Naomi's son (v. 17), possibly because he would inherit through the transfer of Naomi's lands redeemed by Boaz, or because the child was close to Naomi's heart, a comfort that hopefully freed her from her prison of bitter resentment.

These two widows, Naomi and Ruth, demonstrate withholding and giving. One looked only at her lack while the other stepped into the abundance God provides through faith in Him.

Another widow who lived in the abundance mindset that freed her to give is recognized by Jesus.

> He sat down opposite the treasury and watched the people putting money into the offering box. Many rich people put in large sums. And a poor widow came and put in two small copper coins, which make a penny. And he called his disciples to him and said to them, "Truly, I say to you, this poor widow has put in more than all those who are contributing to the offering box. For they all contributed out of their abundance, but she out of her poverty has put in everything she had, all she had to live on." (Mark 12:41–44)

Earlier in that chapter, Jesus had been having ongoing conversations with the Pharisees and Sadducees. He told them the parable of the tenants who kill the vineyard owner's son. The religious leaders also asked Jesus about paying taxes and about marriage at the resurrection as they tried to trap Him in His words.

He reminded His listeners of the greatest commandment—to love God and others. Then He warned against the scribes, "who devour widows' houses and for a pretense make long prayers" (v. 40). This was the setting for the widow who entered and gave all she had.

The rich gave out of their abundant riches, but this poor widow gave out of a mindset of abundance in God. Jesus acknowledged her worldly poverty but commended her for giving despite that. Her choice to give provided more than coins for the treasury; it also served as a contrast to those who withheld their hearts from the God who was about to give them everything—His only Son, Jesus.

> **To choose to give rather than withhold frees us from this world's snares.**

We don't hear any more about this widow. But the graceful influence of her story inspires us all to give. So too with Ruth. Naomi's influence might have ended with the poison of bitterness if it weren't for Ruth's giving heart. Naomi was able to share in Ruth's legacy through Obed, who is in the line of Jesus.

To choose to give rather than withhold frees us from this world's snares and gives us an impact that reaches into eternity.

BIBLE

There is a modern deception that God's hand, through His church, is always out, and that if we start giving, there will be no end to the asking. However, in Exodus 36:1–7, we read that God's people gave so much to the work that God restrained them from giving more. Verse 6 says, "So Moses gave command, and word was proclaimed throughout the camp, 'Let no man or woman do anything more for the contribution for the sanctuary.'"

All that we have, whether we realize it or not, comes from God. What we return to Him, He asks that we give not under compulsion but with joy (2 Corinthians 9:7).

Bible Extra

Another story of abundance involves Elijah and the widow of Zarephath (1 Kings 17:7–16). The widow had nearly run out of flour and oil when the prophet asked her to use the little she had left to make him a cake. When she chose to give, she was rewarded. Rather than cling to what little she had, she provided for the man of God, and her entire household reaped the benefit.

BATTLE

We live in a world that has made idols of money, riches, and luxury. The temptation to envy, hoard, withhold, or embrace resentment is everywhere we turn. This is an essential battle for every believer to recognize and to overcome.

What's the key to resisting the temptation to withhold and live instead with a generous heart and spirit? It's understanding the abundance that is ours in Christ. Reflecting on passages such as Ephesians 1:3–14 can help us focus our minds on all we have in Christ and loosen our grip.

Bottom Line

To choose to give rather than withhold
frees us from this world's snares.

26

Prostitute of Proverbs and Bride of Song of Songs

The Impact of Sexual Restraint

*Her feet go down to death; her steps follow the
path to Sheol; she does not ponder the path of life;
her ways wander, and she does not know it.*

Proverbs 5:5–6

Sex was God's idea.

We know this, and yet we choose to be confused about it all the time.

Our God created some of us to enjoy one another within the context of loving, faithful marriages. He could have designed us to procreate through spores, by cloning cells, or by much less enjoyable processes—just as He might have designed us to receive nourishment through nutritional injections but instead created taste buds and delicious food for us to enjoy.

Sin and evil have distorted both our sexual and physical appetites to disturbing lengths. But individually, we can see His

191

kingdom come in our lives through choosing sexual restraint, whether God's plan for us includes marriage or not.

Discussing sexual restraint invites accusations of promoting prudish, archaic notions. But it's not about short skirts or back seats. Really, it's about promoting a culture of life over a culture of death.

In Proverbs 7, Solomon wrote, "Keep my commandments and live" (v. 2). In this chapter, he described the entrapment of a young man "lacking sense" by a woman lacking in sexual restraint. He described the woman's blatant seduction of the youth. Solomon portrayed her as loud, wayward, sensual, and unashamed of her adultery. No doubt Solomon had significant experience with a great variety of women, having over seven hundred wives and three hundred concubines (1 Kings 11:3).

(Lest you think the Bible places the burden for restraint solely on women, many New Testament passages—Matthew 5:28; 1 Corinthians 6:18; 1 Thessalonians 4:3–5; and Hebrews 13:4; to name some—exhort both sexes to follow God's plan for sexual expression within the context of faithful marriage.)

With stunning similes, Solomon goes on: "All at once he follows her, as an ox goes to the slaughter, or as a stag is caught fast till an arrow pierces its liver; as a bird rushes into a snare; he does not know that it will cost him his life" (Proverbs 7:22–23). Certainly, the young man had a choice in this situation. Solomon used the strongest words to urge him to make the right one. But the woman too had choices.

There is equality throughout Scripture. All are capable of sin, and sin leads to death. Most of us don't experience physical death because of bad daily decisions, but we can destroy relationships and reputations. We can ruin hopes, dreams, and desired outcomes.

Women aren't depicted in Scripture as always innocent, weak, and in need of protection. At times, God demonstrates that women too can be predators. This is how Solomon portrayed women he wanted his son to avoid.

The outcome of such sexual license is, according to Solomon, death. Again, Solomon isn't necessarily describing physical death but death of heart, soul, wholeness, wellness, and relationship with God and others. There's really no need to elaborate on the impact of sexual license on a culture, as we live surrounded by the influence of people who toss aside sexual restraint.

Solomon himself lived unaligned with God's commands for moral restraint. He ignored God's warning to the kings of Israel not to take many wives (Deuteronomy 17:17). Solomon was the likely author of Ecclesiastes (1:1). That author wrote explicitly of his countless regrets. In chasing after unbridled pleasure, he learned that it is all "vanity and a striving after wind" (2:11).

But while Solomon details sexual immorality and provides us with an example of disobedience, he also paints another far more positive portrait of sexuality. In the Song of Solomon, he describes in poetic detail what a healthy, intimate marital relationship looks like. Whereas the woman described in Proverbs 7 chose to cast aside sexual restraint, the bride in Song of Solomon chooses faithfulness, celebrating it and the benefits she experiences solely within her marriage to the king.

Song of Solomon (or Song of Songs) is about more than a relationship between a bride and groom. Many see in it a poetic metaphor for the relationship of the Messiah and His people. Paul told us that marriage is a picture of Jesus and the church.

There is such holiness and meaning infused in this most intimate of relationships and the act of sexual intercourse that to stray from it damages a culture spiritually even more than it does morally. The enemy of God knows this and so works overtime tempting us to abandon God's plan for our sexual expression.

Solomon's bride states, "I adjure you, O daughters of Jerusalem, by the gazelles or the does of the field, that you not stir up or awaken love until it pleases" (Song of Solomon 2:7). In other words, delay gratification until the fullness of time. Don't get ahead of your relationship sexually. Hold back until you are both secure. These are wise and wonderful endorsements for restraint.

The groom speaks of his bride with romantic descriptors and excitement they delayed until the time was right. "You have captivated my heart, my sister, my bride; you have captivated my heart with one glance of your eyes, with one jewel of your necklace. How beautiful is your love, my sister, my bride! How much better is your love than wine, and the fragrance of your oils than any spice!" (4:9–10).

Wine must age. Vintners restrain themselves from indulging before each wine has reached its fullness. The imagery Solomon used here was replete with messages of the reward of sexual restraint.

Part of the deliciously anticipated pleasure of the groom was knowing his bride had chosen this restraint. He proclaims, "A garden locked is my sister, my bride, a spring locked, a fountain sealed" (v. 12).

As the couple meet for their wedding, their words for one another are laden with double meaning, comparing their romance to gardens, flowers, sheep, and fruit. It's clear that while they'd held back from others, they were more than ready to surrender all to one another. "I am my beloved's, and his desire is for me" (7:10).

Restraint, waiting, modesty, fidelity—these are words and notions considered outdated by some today. Still, like ancient relics cast from gold, they have not lost their value just by falling out of fashion. We can retrieve them from history, dust them off, and return them to use to our benefit. To choose sexual restraint is truly to live counterculturally and to have a graceful influence on others for Christ.

In this fallen world, some women's sexual choices are taken from them when they are most vulnerable. This is a tragedy, and the trauma can distort how some women hear and receive even the words of Song of Solomon. We must be gentle with one another when teaching about sexual sin and restraint. Many of us have deep wounds that affect the fullness of our experience in this area of life.

We can pray for healing. We can provide safer spaces for discussing hard history, and terrible hurts. We can strengthen one another and surround younger women—and older single women and widows—with encouragement, company, and inclusion to stave off temptation, self-recrimination, and shame for past mistakes.

Choosing sexual restraint promotes life within marriage and freedom from sexual regrets outside marriage. It promotes relational, emotional, mental, and physical life by reducing our exposure to the many levels of damage that occur when people choose sexual license over God's design.

And for those who have cast off restraint, there is still hope. Jesus met many women who formerly lived like the woman in Proverbs 7 but then found freedom following Him. They demonstrate that we too can make a new decision, a new start, in Jesus, anytime.

As the church, we must live from the sure foundation of this hope and see the image of God in every person, no matter what choices he or she is currently making. Choosing sexual restraint promotes life. Choosing the hope of redemption promotes new life eternal.

BIBLE

Read Song of Solomon over a week (there are eight chapters). Consider the power of the poetic language that celebrates the union between the bride and groom. Compare their relationship with Proverbs 5 and 7.

What is the impact of restraint on relationships before and after marriage, both on couples and on their community? What does the lack of restraint cause in these relationships and in society as a whole? What's the difference between the way the Bible describes sexual restraint and the way it's portrayed in modern culture and the media?

Bible Extra

Read 1 Corinthians 7. Paul discusses singleness, marriage, and work for the Lord. Can you capture his message in one sentence?

Gomer was an unfaithful wife to the prophet Hosea. Through their relationship, God demonstrated His relentless love for unfaithful Israel. "The LORD said to me, 'Go again, love a woman who is loved by another man and is an adulteress, even as the LORD loves the children of Israel, though they turn to other gods and love cakes of raisins'" (Hosea 3:1). Consider what that speaks to your heart about God's love.

BATTLE

It's easy to believe the lie, widely accepted in current thinking, that throwing off sexual restraint is the pathway to freedom. This aligns with what both our sin nature and our natural impatience are telling us. It's little surprise that young people and older adults alike often abandon moral restraint to exercise great license.

It's also no surprise that, rather than freedom, they often find disheartening situations with consequences that continue throughout their lifetimes. But Jesus can heal and restore. When we turn from our sin, repent, and follow His ways, there is no condemnation (Romans 8), and there is freedom (John 8:36).

The sooner we choose sexual restraint, the less the damage done. But we're best off having the biblical image in mind—the benefits of loyalty, trust, self-control, genuine love, and peace, both personal and relational—not the world's image of uptight, repressed, boring prudishness. God's ways lead to life, life in abundance. This can only be found through Jesus.

Bottom Line

Choosing sexual restraint promotes life. Choosing the hope of redemption promotes new life eternal.

27

Priscilla and Jezebel

The Impact of Prophecy (Sound Teaching)

The time is coming when people will not endure sound teaching, but having itching ears they will accumulate for themselves teachers to suit their own passions.

2 Timothy 4:3

The apostles wrote their letters to the believers in the early church during dangerous times. Travel was risky due to robbers. Wars erupted, and life was cheap to those in power. Simple illnesses could lead to death. Famines occurred. Plus, the church faced intense persecution, with believers ejected from the synagogue, shut out from businesses, arrested, and sometimes killed.

And yet, the apostles devoted great portions of their letters to warning Christians to be vigilant about addressing one menace in particular. The greatest threat to the church on the apostolic radar was false teaching or false prophecy—those who promoted it and those who tolerated it.

Throughout the Bible, God uses strong words for false teachers and prophets. The results for those who fall prey to their deception could be eternal.

In Revelation 2:18–29, Jesus addressed the church in Thyatira. He commended the believers there for their works, love, faith, service, and patient endurance. Those are wonderful characteristics for any church to hear about themselves. But there was also a problem, and it centered around a woman. Jesus referred to her as Jezebel.

That may have been her actual name, or Jesus may have called her that to liken her activity to Queen Jezebel, the famous idolater and persecutor of God's prophets in Old Testament times. It's not hard to draw comparisons.

> I have this against you, that you tolerate that woman Jezebel, who calls herself a prophetess and is teaching and seducing my servants to practice sexual immorality and to eat food sacrificed to idols. I gave her time to repent, but she refuses to repent of her sexual immorality. Behold, I will throw her onto a sickbed, and those who commit adultery with her I will throw into great tribulation, unless they repent of her works, and I will strike her children dead. And all the churches will know that I am he who searches mind and heart, and I will give to each of you according to your works. (vv. 20–23)

The Bible likens idolatry to spiritual adultery. We can serve only one God. The church in Thyatira was tolerating a false prophet who compromised the gospel of Jesus. Jesus acknowledged a faithful remnant, but the majority had subjected themselves in some way to her erroneous teaching.

Jezebel was unrepentant. Jesus gave her an opportunity to change her ways. God is merciful, forgiving, and gracious. But Jezebel loved her deception more than she loved the truth. Jesus also gave her followers time to repent, but He promised tribulation in their lives if they refused. Better to suffer briefly and come to repentance than to suffer for eternity. The sin here was not only false prophecy but also tolerating this prophetess and not taking steps to address her lies.

Jezebel's sin was not in identifying as a prophet per se. Women prophets are mentioned in Scripture. Acts 21:8–9 mentions Philip the evangelist's four daughters as prophetesses. Moses's sister, Miriam, was a prophetess (Exodus 15:20). Deborah (Judges 4:4) and Huldah (2 Kings 22:14) were also recognized prophetesses. Scripture calls Isaiah's wife a prophetess (Isaiah 8:3), although wives of prophets were traditionally given that title, and it's unclear if she actually prophesied. Nehemiah mentions opposition from "the prophetess Noadiah" (Nehemiah 6:14).

False teachers and prophets often begin teaching or prophesying God's truth but then twist or corrupt it by injecting deception, either by adding or subtracting from God's Word. Paul warns,

> What I am doing I will continue to do, in order to undermine the claim of those who would like to claim that in their boasted mission they work on the same terms as we do. For such men are false apostles, deceitful workmen, disguising themselves as apostles of Christ. And no wonder, for even Satan disguises himself as an angel of light. So it is no surprise if his servants, also, disguise themselves as servants of righteousness. Their end will correspond to their deeds. (2 Corinthians 11:12–15)

James also cautions, "Not many of you should become teachers, my brothers, for you know that we who teach will be judged with greater strictness" (James 3:1). This is why Jesus speaks with such stern warnings and issues harsh consequences regarding "Jezebel" and those who tolerate her. Her choice to remain unrepentant and to engage in false prophecy demonstrates that she had made an idol of herself and turned from faithfulness to God.

Priscilla and Aquila, on the other hand, were a wife-husband teaching-tentmaking team. Paul, also a tentmaker, stayed with them in Corinth (Acts 18). The couple had relocated there from Rome when Claudius commanded all Jews to leave that city. Later, when Paul left for Ephesus, Priscilla and Aquila traveled with him, remaining in Ephesus to host a church in their home when Paul traveled on.

At the end of Acts 18, we come to understand Priscilla and Aquila's instructional or prophetic role.

> Now a Jew named Apollos, a native of Alexandria, came to Ephesus. He was an eloquent man, competent in the Scriptures. He had been instructed in the way of the Lord. And being fervent in spirit, he spoke and taught accurately the things concerning Jesus, though he knew only the baptism of John. He began to speak boldly in the synagogue, but when Priscilla and Aquila heard him, they took him aside and explained to him the way of God more accurately. (vv. 24–26)

Apollos was a powerful speaker and had some truth of the gospel, but he was incomplete in his knowledge. Priscilla, along with her husband, demonstrated both hospitality and wise instruction to "explain to him the way of God more accurately."

The immediate outcome of her accurate instruction was that Apollos was fully equipped for ministry when he moved on. "And when he wished to cross to Achaia, the brothers encouraged him and wrote to the disciples to welcome him. When he arrived, he greatly helped those who through grace had believed, for he powerfully refuted the Jews in public, showing by the Scriptures that the Christ was Jesus" (vv. 27–28).

Not all believers who teach inaccurate information are trying to be deceptive. Some simply need to sit under more thorough teaching to learn the full message of the gospel of Jesus.

The Priscillas and Aquilas of the church don't ignore wrong teaching or prophecies; they identify them, call them out (with gentleness whenever possible), offer the perpetrator the opportunity to learn the truth, and patiently instruct with accuracy and grace.

Fortunately, we have myriad instructions from the apostles about how to identify and to handle those not teaching God's truth. Paul told Timothy,

> If anyone teaches a different doctrine and does not agree with the sound words of our Lord Jesus Christ and the teaching that accords with godliness, he is puffed up with conceit and understands nothing. He has an unhealthy craving for controversy and for quarrels about words, which produce envy, dissension, slander, evil suspicions, and constant friction among people who are depraved in mind and deprived of the truth, imagining that godliness is a means of gain. (1 Timothy 6:3–5)

Repeatedly, the New Testament writers warn us to be on our guard against wrongful teaching or false prophets—to know they will come and to be looking and prepared to spot them. Clearly, as we see in Jesus's warning to Thyatira, we're not to tolerate false prophecies in our faith communities but must deal with false teaching as sin.

We have strong examples of ministry in the early church. Priscilla stands out as one who chose sound teaching and accurate prophecy. Leaders of the early church were willingly accountable to one another, setting a strong example of mutual submission. Most missionaries worked in teams, and anyone straying from the truth was corrected.

Jesus's words about Jezebel of Thyatira present a daunting picture of the influence of her false prophecy. The graceful influence of Priscilla's (and her husband's) sound teaching is seen at least in the fortification of Apollos's ministry. But we're sure to see it had even greater impact when we're together in glory.

BIBLE

In Acts 20:28–31, Paul tells the leaders of the Ephesian church,

> Pay careful attention to yourselves and to all the flock, in which the Holy Spirit has made you overseers, to care for the church of God, which he obtained with his own blood. I know that after my departure fierce wolves will come in among you, not sparing the flock; and from among your own selves will arise men speaking twisted things, to draw away the disciples after them. Therefore be alert, remembering that for three years I did not cease night or day to admonish every one with tears.

Paul set the example of praying without ceasing for the churches, teaching truth, correcting error, and addressing false teachers and prophets. The warnings against false teaching are mentioned by all the writers of the New Testament epistles. Why is this danger mentioned more than arrest or persecution by those who hated the church?

Bible Extra

The book of Jude is only one chapter, and its theme is false teachers. Read it and make a list of what you learn about false teaching from this letter.

BATTLE

In today's information age, false teaching or false prophecy can spread faster and in more forms than we can fathom. False prophets are often driven by financial gain (1 Timothy 6:3–10). It is wise, then, for those of us who are gifted in teaching, speaking, or prophesying to watch our attitudes toward financial gain and to remain accountable to others for our teaching. Priscilla and Aquila's teamwork as a couple is a wonderful model, but we can also team with friends, coworkers, or church leaders.

Paul warns, "Keep a close watch on yourself and on the teaching. Persist in this, for by so doing you will save both yourself and your hearers" (1 Timothy 4:16). We can't imagine that any of us is beyond temptation to stray from God's truth, especially the closer we come to the second coming of Christ, when deception will be so rampant. We need one another to help us stand firm in choosing wise instruction and in guarding against false prophecy and false teachers.

Bottom Line

The greatest threat to the church on the apostolic radar was false teaching and false prophecy—those who promoted it and those who tolerated it.

The Woman Who Was Not Hidden

The Impact of Reaching Out to Jesus

*Do not pronounce judgment before the time, before the
Lord comes, who will bring to light the things now hidden
in darkness and will disclose the purposes of the heart.
Then each one will receive his commendation from God.*

1 Corinthians 4:5

We all know about that one woman not yet mentioned in this book. The one who was hurting. The one who felt different and left out. The one who stood alone.

Amid a throng of people, despite the crowd, despite her troubles, despite the exclusion she'd experienced, and the damage people had done to her spirit, despite all that, she found the courage to believe that if she just reached out to Jesus, she would receive from Him what she needed.

So she did.

She chose to reach out to Jesus.

She thought what she'd done would go unnoticed. She thought

she would remain invisible and simply, quietly, receive what she needed.

But Jesus called her out. "Someone touched me, for I perceive that power has gone out from me" (Luke 8:46).

"And when the woman saw that she was not hidden, she came trembling, and falling down before him declared in the presence of all the people why she had touched him, and how she had been immediately healed" (v. 47).

She saw that she was not hidden.

That woman is you.

You are not hidden.

Jesus has called you out.

You may not have a physical ailment like the bleeding woman mentioned in Luke 8:40–54. You may have been raised in a Christian home. Or maybe you weren't.

You may have struggled with addiction, cutting, or living promiscuously. Or maybe you struggled with perfectionism, legalism, or a judgmental heart.

You may have experienced abuse, or you may have rebelled against people who loved you. Or maybe you have just quietly grown up feeling a little out of place, a little alone, and very unseen.

Whatever your life experience, at some point, you encountered Jesus. Even though He was about His work and busy with many people, something in your spirit told you that He also had something for you.

So, like the bleeding woman, you acted on the faith that appeared in your heart like a candle in a dark room. You reached out. You touched the hem of His garment.

He stopped.

He turned.

You finally understood that you weren't invisible after all. Jesus sees you.

You invited Him into your heart. You accepted His sacrifice

as payment for your sins. You gave Him your life and entered an eternal relationship with the Creator of the universe.

That prayer you prayed, that step you took, it seems like such a small act, like touching the hem of His robe. And yet, in the moment it happened, you stepped into the start of your new, eternal life.

Life lived in His light. Unhidden. Seen.

He made an eternal impact on you.

And now, out of love for Him, you've desired to have a graceful influence in His name.

You are already doing it.

You are an influencer.

Your life has impact.

Our greatest problem is not that our lives don't matter. It's that they do. It's not that we're insignificant; it's that our significance is hidden from us.

It's not hard to imagine that the woman who had been bleeding for twelve years may have let her condition and other people's treatment of her convince her that she didn't matter.

Perhaps by calling her out, Jesus was indicating that He wanted to heal her of more than her physical issue. He wanted to heal her of her fear that she was invisible, that her life didn't matter.

> **Our greatest problem is not that our lives don't matter. It's that they do.**

Sin, evil, and our own self-doubt hide from us the power of a single life. But then we reach out to Jesus, and we realize we are not hidden.

When we touch Jesus in faith, power goes out from Him to us.

He influences us. We influence others.

C. S. Lewis wrote in *The Weight of Glory*, "There are no *ordinary* people. You have never talked to a mere mortal. Nations, cultures, arts, civilisations—these are mortal, and their life is to ours as the life of a gnat. But it is immortals whom we joke with, work with, marry, snub and exploit—immortal horrors or ever-lasting splendours."[9]

You've probably observed what I've noticed in researching the women's stories for this book. God used the godly choices women made to change their lives and those around them for decades, sometimes centuries, and often for eternity.

Those who made ungodly choices found their impact cut short or limited mostly to their own lifetimes, although sins such as idolatry and false teaching can have eternal implications for others.

Our actions can influence generations of those who come after us, but God is merciful.

> You shall not make for yourself a carved image, or any likeness of anything that is in heaven above, or that is on the earth beneath, or that is in the water under the earth. You shall not bow down to them or serve them; for I the LORD your God am a jealous God, visiting the iniquity of the fathers on the children to the third and fourth generation of those who hate me, but showing steadfast love to thousands of those who love me and keep my commandments. (Deuteronomy 5:8–10)

Some women who initially made ungodly decisions repented and found they could still receive forgiveness and new life from God. God has infinite mercy for those who repent and turn to Him. While we live, there is every reason to hope.

While we live, there is every reason for others to pray that each of us will reach out to Jesus and find our eternity gracefully influenced by His love and life.

There are many women mentioned in the New Testament about which we know very little—Apphia, Junia, Nereus's sister, and Claudia, to name a few. We don't learn their stories. We don't receive information about their choices, except one: we know they chose to follow Jesus. And that was enough for God to make sure you and I would realize He knew them by name. They were not hidden. They were chosen.

And so are we.

Each of us may be living amid a mix of godly and ungodly behaviors—ours and others'. But the result of choosing Jesus, reaching out to Him, and receiving the healing that salvation brings, means we will outlive all sins when we step into eternity. We will be out of reach of the sins of others. We will fully experience the freedom we inherit in Jesus Christ.

We experience a measure of that freedom now when we choose Jesus, live for Jesus, and make decisions informed by obedience to His Word and the prompting of the Holy Spirit. We ask for His kingdom to come—into our hearts, lives, and thinking—and it does.

We are not hidden. We are seen, and in Christ we are free to make godly choices that shape our lives and gracefully influence the lives of those around us with life, light, and eternal hope.

We just reach out to Jesus, and when He calls us, we answer.

BIBLE

Read the story of the bleeding woman in Luke 8:42–48. Why do you think she didn't immediately speak up when Jesus asked who touched Him? What was so important for her, and for us, about her coming forward and declaring "in the presence of all the people why she had touched him, and how she had been immediately healed" (v. 47)?

Bible Extra

Read these verses: Psalms 33:18; 139:13–16; Jeremiah 12:3; Proverbs 15:3. Consider the implications of knowing we are not hidden from God at any time. How is this encouraging and motivating?

BATTLE

It's easy to imagine we're so small and insignificant as individuals that we convince ourselves our choices have little impact. It's especially difficult when our lives aren't going the way we want them to go. We wonder: If we can't control the aspects of our lives that are being challenged, what difference does any of our effort make?

And yet, Jesus tells us He has a plan and purpose for each of us. He sees us. Loves us. Redeems us. "You are a chosen race, a royal priesthood, a holy nation, a people for his own possession, that you may proclaim the excellencies of him who called you out of darkness into his marvelous light" (1 Peter 2:9).

He has called us out. We are not hidden. Our decisions can reach into eternity by His power and grace. Trusting this helps us live well, speak truth, and minister to others in His name, knowing our actions have far-reaching implications for us and for many others.

Bottom Line

You are not hidden. You have lasting impact. You
are a graceful influence in the power of Jesus.

Acknowledgments

To the amazing team at Our Daily Bread Publishing. To the team who prays for every writer, reader, and word. To Dawn Anderson, Sarah De Mey, Robert Hartig, Melissa Wade, and everyone who contributed to make this book the best it could be for the kingdom. Thank you from the depths of this writer's heart.

To Bob Hostetler, agent, friend, brother in Christ, lover of puns. Your pastoral heart shows in all you do. You inspire me to excellence in writing and in faith. Truly, thank you.

To Steve Laube, thank you for listening to my ideas and letting me know which ones are just terrible. Thank you for being kind enough to be honest and for making time to give me wise counsel over this past year. Your giant heart is not hidden.

To Pastor Jim Menzies, thank you for patiently (even enthusiastically) answering all my Bible and theology questions. I'm forever grateful that you stand between me and heresy!

To my writing family from EZ Writers to Light Brigade, Blue Ridge to Renew, Sabbath Writers to my Take Heart! and Persevere coaching clients, and all the writers in between, you have truly kept me writing even when it seemed impossible. Never, never give up. Let us drop our pens as we take His hand home.

To my church family at First Baptist Church in Hope Valley (especially the Bible study ladies), thank you for loving me so well and for not minding when I bring taco chips and salsa to potlucks!

To Kathy for every phone call, visit, and encouragement. Thank you for sharing my life. You keep me honest and prevent me from being friendless. I'm so glad we have forever to be friends.

To Rob, Zack, Jess, Hannah, Andrew, Logan, Christian, Sam, and Wade, you are my beating heart. Your lasting impact on my life will always be love, joy, and belonging. Being your wife, mother, mother-in-law, and Omi keeps me excited about life on this outpost of glory.

Finally, to all the women in all the Bible studies around the globe, thank you for keeping the faith by digging into God's Word. You shine His light in a dark world. Persevere until He comes.